THE STREET MUSICIAN

Written By:

BILL RICHARDSON

Acknowledgements

Edited by M. J. Brown

Illustrations and Graphics by M. J. Brown

Photographer, Ashley Reynolds

Special Thanks to William and Laura Richardson

TABLE OF CONTENT

PROLOGUE

The uniqueness of this book portrays a tradition of music performance that cultivated from the bowels of New Orleans called *Street Music*. This type of entertainment grew right along with other identifying genres of American Music, particularly jazz and blues, which has been accepted in every American Society and throughout the world as the greatest music of all times.

New Orleans, the home of the Choctaw and Natchez Indians, was well known for its streets of marching bands belching out the sounds of good music before there was the phenomenon of jazz. The Creoles played music particularly based on French customs, and the Cuban-African rhythm was also a part of that musical mixture. The White musicians were the ones who would play music on the streetcars. They could set up tents along the busy areas of the city and could march the streets in Bands. The Black people performed their African music in a designated area using their handmade African drums and string instruments. Song and dance played a major part in the social gatherings of the people of New Orleans. Back in the day, they would gather in a place called the Congo Square[1], a grassy plain on the northwestern edge of the city where slave owners permitted slaves to sing and dance for a few hours on Sundays. After the Blacks in the city were freed from slavery they began to combine their musical mixture with the use of European instruments, particularly brass and woodwind. Soon they also began to march the streets and gather at the park sites with their own form of music[2].

There is very little history written precisely on street music, however it is well included in the documentation of American music development. Today, street music has grown into a professional practice, whereby musicians perform on the streets as bands and individual musicians to earn a living. While New Orleans is most renowned for this tradition,

---

[1] The Congo Square was eventually shut down due to slave owners who feared that their African slaves were communicating with each other through the beats of their drums.
[2] *Jazz: A History Of American Music,* by Geoffrey C. Ward and Ken Burns

street music has now traveled to most major cities such as Chicago, New York, Washington D.C and San Francisco, as well as far away cities, such as Amsterdam, Holland, and Paris, France.

There isn't much, if any, culture of street music in the city of St. Louis, Missouri. The musicians have not established this as a way of life, or as a part of music performance. However, during the earlier part of the 19th Century and during the 50's and 60"s, there was street music in St. Louis. The street style of musical performance lack of support from St. Louisans, businesses, and passersby encountered legal ramifications and was eventually outlawed and abandoned by street performing musicians. *Street Music* became synonymous to *peace disturbance* when not wanted around.

Today, there is a hand-full of musicians who are carrying out this tradition of performance in St. Louis. They perform in eventful areas, particularly The Delmar Loop where musicians sit along the busy sidewalks of Delmar Boulevard (The Loop) playing their instruments and taking donations of appreciations. The Edwards Jones Dome also attracts some street performers during the football season, as well as the Busch Stadium during baseball season. Many of these musicians travel from the city of Chicago to perform in St. Louis at the baseball and football games. They favor St. Louis because they are up against very little competition, as opposed to their home town where street entertainment is very prevalent.

St. Louis has paved the way in American Music History for many years. Beginning with the influential music of W.C. Handy, "Father of the Blues", and the Great Scott Joplin, "The King of Ragtime", whose popular rags, especially *The Maple Leaf Rag* and *The Entertainer*, paved the way for American Pop Music. Then, there is the Great Chuck Berry[3], "The father of Rock n' Roll", and one of the greatest innovators of all times! A true original, Berry has produced some of the best songs ever written showcasing his electrifying style and rhythmic guitar. Combining that with his stimulating moves in the creation of his most

---

[3] "While no individual can be said to have invented rock and roll, Berry arguably did more than anyone else to put the pieces together. As rock journalist Dave Marsh wrote, Chuck Berry is to rock and roll what Louis Armstrong is to Jazz." Excerpt from *Chuck Berry Biography*, Rock –n-Roll Hall Of Fame, The Inductees.

popular dance, *The Duck Walk*, Chuck Berry brought about musical change! There was an outpour of happiness and massive good times throughout the country and the world when his music hit the airwaves. He was able to bring people together unlike anyone had done before him.

With Musical Greats such as these, there is no wonder why St. Louis is well known throughout the countryside as the home of rhythm and blues, which is the backbone of American Music.

INTRODUCTION

The essence of this book is based on the real life story of a musician who plays on the streets of St. Louis Missouri. Through an intertwining of narratives and poems, the author weaves for you a glimpse into the days of his life. For a period of time he was strung out on drugs and homeless. It was during his recovery that he began to gather material to write a book based on his life, the life of a *Street Musician*. His mind became very clear, focused and free of drugs. He relates music to his everyday life with jaw dropping chronicles of things he actually witnessed and lived through. The main character is real and his experiences of being a street musician is what he lived. Some fictional points and character developments have been added to highlight the story.

This story portrays the perseverance and dedication of two musicians, their similarities and differences, their commitments and dreams, their compassion for others and the sacrifices it takes to get what you want out of life. It's a story of two people finding each other by chance, or by the timely hand of fate.

The author learned about the fascinations and wonderful cultures of street music during his travels as a musician, in cities such as New York, Chicago and New Orleans. After growing accustomed to playing with bands in the club scenes, he decided that he wanted to do something different. He began to play music in the streets. And like the ticking hands of time with sand sifting through an hourglass, grind-by-grind, day-by-day, month after month and eventually, over the years, his life style cultivated into the life of The Street Musician.

THE STREET MUSICIAN

Chapter 1

DOWNTOWN

The wonderful sounds of music filled the air of downtown St. Louis, echoing against the towering brick walls of buildings. The streets were filled with cars and trucks that seemed to move along in rhythmic progression, crossing slowly into the intersections as if bouncing to a beat. Pedestrians seemed to dance along the busy sidewalks, crowding the corners, waiting for the stoplights to turn green and flash the bright, white display of WALK. The floor to ceiling windows were decorated with beautiful furniture, fashionable clothing, sparkling jewelry, and pictures of art. Large neon signs hung above the buildings and on the glass display of storefronts. Department stores, restaurants, hotels, and many places of business lined the sidewalks.

From a near distance the chime of bells could be heard along with the easy flow of music that continued to penetrate the busy atmosphere with a delightful sound. It was 12:00, noon, an ordinary day, but a special time for the office and store workers and early shoppers moving in and out, creating a rush hour of congestion. It was lunchtime.

It was a hot summer afternoon as the beaming sun smiled down onto the city from the clear, blue sky through white pillowing clouds that looked like huge cotton balls. Bill looked out among the crowd of people and the traffic of automobiles as he stood in the dense, blue shadow of the red brick building that sat on the corner of 7th Street and Olive Street. The ambiance of music that enchanted the heart of downtown St. Louis came from the deep bell of his saxophone. He was a musician who played on the streets of the city, demonstrating tremendous talent and skill, but what came out of his saxophone was literally the story of his life. People dropped donations into his duffel bag as they passed by. Sometimes they requested particular songs and artists. He enjoyed playing the songs by *Frank Sinatra, Duke Ellington, Billie Holiday, Grover Washington, David Sanborn, Kenny* G the most, but he didn't mind the requests. He even played classics by *Beethoven* and ragtime by *Scott Joplin.*

After more than an hour of serenading the scene, he noticed the traffic of people becoming thin. He glanced at his watch. It was 1:30 P.M., the end of another afternoon of music. He removed the donations from his bag and placed the money into a black pouch. Then, he carefully placed the saxophone into the duffel bag. It was a perfect size for the instrument. He slung the gunny sack like bag across his shoulder and began to walk down the street. It was now his lunch hour.

He went through the doors of the Red Door Chinese Restaurant located on Olive Street. A woman behind the counter asked, "May I help you?" He immediately ordered a carry out of special fried rice with a cold beverage. "That will be six dollars and fifty cents," The woman said. Bill fished his left hand into his pants pocket and counted out seven single dollar-bills. He placed them on the wooden counter. The woman quickly tilled the register and handed Bill his change. There was a red oriental chair behind him. He looked around as he sat down to wait for his order. The walls were beautifully decorated with designs and pictures that gave the room an oriental feel as you inhale the pleasant and familiar aroma of Chinese food.

An elderly lady approached him with a radiant smile. He immediately recognized her as a fan, a woman that he has played songs for. She worked for the downtown St. Louis Public Library and often spoke to Bill about her studies of the Chinese language. Some of her favorite requests for Bill to play were songs such as *The Glory of Love, Strangers in the Night,* and *Autumn Leaves.* Bill respectfully called her *momma.* "Hello there," she said. "I could hear you as I sat here eating my lunch." I had planned to pass by you once I had finished, but miraculously here you are." She pressed several bills into his hand. He thanked her in return with a warm smile.

Bill's order was up and he left out of the restaurant to go find himself a quiet table to eat his lunch outside in Kiener Plaza. The park, seated in the heart of downtown St. Louis, attracted many office workers, tourists and locals, as well as homeless people who dwelled in the area. It was very well kept with a beautiful layer of green decorated with an elaborate waterfall tumbling down marble stairs that glistened from the light of sunrays. At night the illumination effects of colorful halogen lights with the glimmer of water made the view breathtaking.

Throughout the year, rallies, festivals and parades would start or end or start and end at this park. During some of those celebrations Bill would come out and play his saxophone for donations. It was a great and easy way to rake in extra money.

Bill just sat for a while taking in the sights before he began to eat. He noticed the people scattered around the plaza. Some were throwing breadcrumbs feeding the birds. Some looked to be relaxing on the park benches reading the morning paper. There were the homeless, sitting and idling their time away as well as young lovers stealing time in the day to dance in the sun.

These peaceful moments in the park gave Bill the opportunity to rest and gather his thoughts. There was a major event that evening. The Cardinals had a baseball game at Busch Stadium against the New York Giants later. The baseball games were Bill's sense of security. He always did very well in donations. St. Louis Baseball attracted thousands and thousands of people and was the most rewarding event of all for him. Of course, everyone did not make a donation, but his rewards were very handsome.

Bill felt very energetic after eating. After drinking the cool, refreshing beverage he purchased at the restaurant, he placed the empty containers in the trash receptor beside him. He respected the cleanliness of the park. He slung the duffel bag across his shoulder and headed towards Broadway Boulevard to his next destination, The Riverfront.

Chapter 2

THE RIVERFRONT

The Riverfront was crawling with people moving along the paths of walkways. You could see the crowds of people weaving in and out of each other, some bumping and dodging along the way. Others had the heads in the air, looking towards the sky. 630 feet high in the air was the top of the main attraction on the Riverfront. The iconic, clad in stainless steel *Gateway Arch* stands symbolizing the westward expansion of the United States. Another attraction was The Gateway Arch Riverboats. The Becky Thatcher and the Tom Sawyer are a couple of the main boats that sail a distance of the river valley, providing the guest with the great history along the region of the Mississippi River. There was the Helicopter Flight that flew tourists on private rides in close proximity to the river. There were also various stands of venues selling commodities such as snacks, beverages, scarves, necklaces, designer sports caps, and T-shirts, along with trinkets of figures representing the heritage and spirit of St. Louis. It is a most enjoyable time.

Bill chose to sit on a concrete bench across from the grand stairway that led to the upper ground level of the Arch. He actually enjoys sitting on the stairs better because the tourist tended to travel the stair path frequently. The position of the stairs projected the music from his saxophone onto the crowded street below, which reflected a reverberating, or echoing sound onto the wide splashing river. It made people notice him and being noticed brings the cash.

Unfortunately for Bill however, the Forrest Rangers, who patrolled the grounds of the Arch, ran him off from the stairs months ago. They explained to him that he could not play and solicit donations because the Gateway Arch was federal property and the Federal Government does not give permits to solicit on their property. This explanation could possibly have been reasonable except for the fact that the drivers of the horse and carriages are allowed to park on the Riverfront and solicit. They have been given permission to park there daily and solicit their services to the public. The rangers suggested that Bill play across the street on the side of the river because it was state property where they had no jurisdiction. The deputies that governed the state property of the Riverfront welcomed his talent, and showed their appreciation. They recognized the added enjoyment Bill's music provided to the tourists. The inequality was so apparent that if *Ray Charles* was still living he could have told Bill that this situation appears to be unfair. But, since he's no longer with us, *Stevie Wonder* stepped in as his back-up. The rule of not soliciting on federal property should apply *fairness to all and not just some*.

Bill recalled one day as he was walking down the Arch steps, he saw two elderly women at the bottom. One was in a wheel chair. When he reached them one of the women asked him if he knew where the accommodations to assist the disabled and elderly up the flight of stairs. Bill said that there was an elevator in the parking garage, but it was not close by. He could not recall there being any accommodations close by. The elderly lady introduced herself and said to Bill that her mother was in the wheelchair. "I can't believe that the Federal Government did not include accommodations to assist the elderly and disabled when they built this tremendous flight of stairs," the lady said. "They surely make every other place of business have accommodations." *Fairness should apply to all of us, not just to some*." She then asked Bill if he could carry the wheel chair up the flight of stairs while she helped her mother make it up. As they walked up the stairs Bill wondered where the Rangers were so that they could assist the two women. He said to himself that they were probably peeping through the eye of a camera to see if the women gave him any money.

When Bill and the two elderly ladies reached the top of the stairs they thanked him for his kindness. He then walked back down the flight of stairs and sat on a bench across the street from the Gate Way Arch by the Tom Sawyer Cruise Boat. The cruise boat was out rolling on the river, but he could hear its whistle close by. He began to play his sax as he waited for the boat to come in.

As Bill sat in the afternoon air waiting on passersby, he played the tune *They Can't Take That Away From Me*. Something seemed off, Bill thought, so he stopped to examine his horn. It wasn't working properly. He flipped it around, looking at his saxophone very closely. He was able to quickly diagnose the problem. It was another broken spring. This time it was the spring that held the F key in position. He immediately remedied it with a rubber band. He had made many home repairs on his saxophone, and lately they were becoming very frequent. There were several rubber bands stretching along the surface of his brass. His horn was very old and antique with a tarnished appearance. It was a German model made in the 1930's with very elaborate and beautiful engravings enveloping the bell. It produced the most sweetest of sound. It rang like a church bell.

Very often you would see saxophone players with an old appearing horn. They understood that over many years of usage the resonance of sound settles into the metal affecting the sound with a particular quality and depth. However, his saxophone needed a complete overhaul and he hoped that one day soon he would eventually earn enough money to afford the high cost of repair.

He began to play the Spanish melody called *Europa*, a very enthralling song made popular by guitarist *Carlos Santana*. People began looking for the beautiful melodious flow. They began to give donations. Children began to smile and dance. He played a personalized version of *Twinkle Twinkle Little Star* followed by *Camp Town Races*, *Pop Goes the Weasel*, *Proud Mary* and then the calypso rhythm of *The Limbo Stick*.

Suddenly, there was a woman standing in front of him holding a little child's hand. The child was holding a dollar in the other hand. The woman greeted Bill. She said that she was a musician who played piano, but loved the sound of the saxophone. Bill stopped playing and said to the woman that he loved the sound of the piano. The little boy looked up at the woman and said, "Momma, I thought you weren't supposed to talk to strangers?" Bill and the mother broke into laughter at what the child had said. Bill looked at the woman with a wide smile and said, "He surely got you that time." 'You aren't supposed to talk to strangers' is the message that most parents instill in their children. Bill then turned and spoke to the child. "What do you want to hear little fellow," he said. "What can I play for you?" Bill subconsciously began to think of the many children songs he knew. The woman said, "Tell him what you want to hear, Tracy." The child looked up at Bill and said, "Play *Hit the*

Road Jack!" Bill was taken by surprise and overwhelmed with laughter again at the child's song request. This song was a hit made by *Ray Charles*, an adult song that he never would have expected a child to request. He played the song and continued to laugh. Sometimes children, he thought, can say the cutest little things.

He had been playing his saxophone for two hours on the Riverfront. Now, it was time to bring the late afternoon of entertainment to an end. He concluded with a ballad by *Ray Charles* titled *You Don't Know Me*. It was time to take a break and get ready for an evening of baseball. He took his instrument apart and placed it into the duffel bag. He grabbed the duffel bag, but as he turned around towards the street, he was suddenly startled. He was face to face with a beautiful woman who was standing very close to him. He stepped back a few feet to allow space between them. She was dressed in a blue, satin jogging suit with matching tennis shoes. She wore a sweatband around her head. Her hair was a reddish brown, like October leaves, woven into long braids with inter-winding, colorful beads and jewels of glitter projecting the image of a majestic crown, a Princess in a fairytale. As he gazed into her mellow, beautiful, seducing cat of eyes it seemed for a moment that he was captivated by a dream. Her pucker of lips was very sensuous and painted with a glistening, red coat of lipstick. Her skin was like chewy, golden, caramel candy. There was a lovely diamond necklace around her sleek of neck that fell into her voluptuous bosom. Bill thought to himself, "Man, what a pretty woman."

"What's up dude?" Bill bobbed his head in acknowledgement with a smile. "Are you finished playing?" the woman continued. "I only heard a little bit of you and you sounded amazing. I came over here to give you a donation and listen longer, but it appears that you're ready to go." Her pronunciation was very articulate. Her voice was sweetly feminine and calm, like a bird of song. Bill said, "Yes, I had packed up to leave, but I can take my saxophone out and play for you." The woman said, "No, you don't have to. Here's the donation, anyway." She handed Bill a twenty-dollar bill. He was impressed with the amount of money. Most of the bills he received in donations were one dollar bills with a few fives here and there. He put it into his pants pocket. "Thank you very much," Bill said. "Well", the woman said, "My name is Marlys. I'm a musician, too. I sing and play the piano. Do you play here often?" Bill said, "Yes, I play this spot a couple of times a week, especially if there is an event going on. I play other major events throughout the city," he continued. "I also give music lessons at my home." "Oh yea?" she exclaimed. "My children are students of music. What kind of instruments do you teach?" "I teach band instruments, the flute, clarinet, trumpet, snare drum and of course the saxophone," he said. "I also teach piano." "My children take private lessons in Creve Coeur," the woman said. "However, their teacher is a very busy person and cancels their lessons much too often for my taste. I'm defiantly in the market to find a new teacher. Maybe, I can I call on you? Do you have a business card?" Bill said, "Of course!" He reached into his pants pocket, pulled out his wallet and handed her a business card. He said, "I'll give you an excellent deal... and also, I perform for special occasions and private parties, if you ever have an event you need entertainment for." That's great," she replied, "because I'm planning a private party in the near future. I'll be in touch."

She extended her slender, luxuriously manicured, diamond ring of hand out for him to shake. He grasped it with his right hand feeling the warm femininity of her soft, tender skin. He kissed it gently. He didn't want to let go. Once again, he gazed into her mellow and dreamy hypnotic eyes. She is surely someone special, he thought to himself. "Who is she?" he pondered. She said, "We'll see each other again." She blew out to him an innocent kiss, but to him it felt like a long, woo of wet kisses from her palm of hand. Then, she turned around and walked away.

Chapter 3

FIRE IN THE HOLE

The neon lights of The Pageant Concert Nightclub gleamed brightly along the east end of The Delmar Loop. The huge parking lot in the back of the theater was filled with cars, SUVs and trucks, while the front was lined with long Limousines, stretched Mercedes Benz's and Porches. The Halo Bar, attached to the front of it was filled with happy people toasting up the night. A hot dog stand on wheels stood in front on the sidewalk catering to people walking along the streets of the Delmar and to the thin line of fans that had begun to exit the show.

The Queen of Venus, St. Louis's number one recording artist, had been the headliner at The Pageant that evening. She was singing her last song of that evening's performance, the big hit from her hot CD: Fire In The Hole!

FIRE IN THE HOLE

They call me party girl….

…..Because I like to dance

Bouncing my hips like a rubber band

Dancing in the street that's what I love

Under the moon in the sky

And under the stars above

The music and my body Is like a plug in a electric sock

People want to know

What makes my body so hot

Fire in The hole is burning through my soul

I can't stop that Fire in the hole

Fire in the hole makes me want to lose control

Can you put out the fire in the hole

Driving down the street in my Pink Mercedes

All dressed up like a sophisticated lady

I pulled up to the hip-hop spot

Pulled off my clothes and Climbed up to the hood top

Black heels with a golden G-string

Red dots on my panty hose

Rosy blotches on my cheeks and

Diamonds on my cute nose

Then, I started shaking everything I got!

People wanted to know what makes my body so hot

Fire in The hole is burning through my soul

I can't stop that Fire in the hole

Fire in the hole makes me want to lose control

Can you put out the fire in the hole

You think you know what to do for me

But, I don't want that kind of romance

I'd like to take you home with me

But, all I want to do is dance

Dancing really turns me on

Good loving isn't what I've been told

So maybe you can understand

I don't want to lose control

People crowd around me throwing money down

When I dance and spread that hip-hop beat around

Some people come to see me because

They want to take a chance

Some people come to see me cause

They think I'm just a quick romance

Some people think that I am just

A piece of hip-hop trash

But, when I bend over

See if you can kiss my ass

Some people come to join in on the fun of hip-hop

Some people want to know what makes my body so hot

Fire in The hole is burning through my soul

I can't stop that Fire in the hole

Fire in the hole

Makes me want to lose control

Can you put out the

Fire in the hole

The packed audience stood and gave a warm round of applause as *The Queen of Venus*, blew kisses from the palms of her red gloved hands. While the crowd continued to cheer to her grand performance, the band played into a hip-hop beat, and the *Queen* exited the stage. She went directly to her dressing room where she waited for the crowd to die down from the excitement of the night. She removed the golden crown from her head and wiped her face with a towel. She took off the clothes she performed in and changed into a comfortable, elegant outfit in preparation to greet the many guests and fans that had gathered backstage. An ornamental chair was placed outside of her dressing room where she soon took a seat and began to greet a long line of acquaintances and fans. She had mastered the concept of appeasing her audience off stage, as well as on stage. She was a real natural in her artistry.

Chapter 4

SWEET HOME

It was a hot summer's night[4] as Bill relaxed inside of his apartment, located on North Broadway Boulevard near the downtown area of St. Louis. In the next block was Smoki 0's Barbecue Grill. Bill ordered many takeout meals here between his ventures and trails of playing street music. Smoki O's was so conveniently located that Bill could easily make it up the steps to his apartment to consume his food while it was still hot. Across the street was a plant that produced and packaged cleaning and sanitation products.   In the block west of his apartment was M & L Frozen Foods, a food and service company that has been providing St. Louis area bars, schools and hotels with food Since 1978. This section of Broadway was scattered with many small businesses and warehouses that had survived from the days gone by when North Broadway boomed with city industries and franchises. Today, the remaining old German buildings give a very gloomy appearance to the quiet neighborhood. He laid in the comfort of his queen size bed absorbed in a very compelling dream of a place where the joy of happiness and peace was infinitely obtainable… fantasia!

---

[4] One Hot Summer Night, *page 153*

The loud and irritating sounds of beeping horns and traffic moving up and down the streets, embarking on a busy work day ripped Bill awake from his dream. He sat straight up in his bed and felt as though all his senses were awake! He could smell the best aromas either coming from the restaurants nearby, or maybe it's old Ms. Turner next door, having a visit from her daughter and grandchild again. She always cooks up the best soul food spread when they come around. His nostrils flared up and his eyes rolled to the back of his head at the thought. He looked around him to make sure of his surroundings. He felt the hairs on his arm stand up and he noticed his heartbeat quicken. He had only been up for a few seconds, but he still felt the emotions of his dream. He remembered it, too. It was of that woman, the beautiful Princess whom he had met on the Riverfront. The breeze from the nearby Mississippi River coming through the crack in his open window allowed him to catch his breath. He plopped his head back down on his pillow. He could still hear his beating heart through the cushion under his head. He felt fatigued and wished to sleep for one or two more hours, but he knew that he had to get up. Music was his method of stimulation, so he began to recite a musical poem:

LET ME GET UP

Let me get up and do my thang
Before my sunshine turns to rain
Let me get up and become a busy man today
No time for fun No time for play
Let me get up like an armored soldier
Mounted on a white stallion horse
As I speak of universal peace
The winds of the world will re-sound
my bellow Of musical voice
Bringing joy to the people As my claim of plan
My dreams are of a music man
Let me get up and soar my message of truth
Like a gigantic bird with flailing wings flight
As the warm, breathily caresses of
wisdom and love
Woo with dancing rhythm of escape
From my musical saxophone
of golden pipe

21

After getting dressed and before leaving his apartment, Bill grabbed his horn from his closet and his business license from the corner mantle. The City Street Department had recently provided him with a license that permits the performance of his street music on city property. This was his protection from the cops, and it made his line of work a legitimate profession. Some venues still gave him problems though, requesting that he "remove himself from in front of their establishments." The attitudes of some of these proprietors who insisted on regarding him as a panhandler caused him to become very resentful. They tried to claim to own the city sidewalks and even parts of the street. Some went as far as to request him to prove he was at a distance of one foot away according to law. Bill knew his rights and when they were wrong he refused to be bullied. The City Street Department provided regulations and guidelines pertaining to street entertainers who purchased a permit, and Bill knew many proprietors were not familiar with the guidelines. An eight inch perimeter around the edge of the sidewalk is owned by the city giving solicitors, advocates and musicians the right to demonstrate and perform within the designated boundaries. There is the possibility that a section of the sidewalk and street may be rented from the city for valet parking by businesses, such as the Hyatt Hotel downtown on Broadway. However, the Crown Hotel located in the next block north of the Hyatt has similar sidewalk and street property set-up accommodations and gives no opposition or complaint to street music. The Edward Jones Dome and the Busch Stadium sidewalk properties may be privately owned or rented because of the complete brick pavement and sidewalk name engravings of famous athletes.

Regardless, Bill would politely comply to these businesses sometimes mockery of requests to move, for he was willing to negotiate the situation. He also knew that whatever their ploy may be, they could not stop the music. It resounds and travels to far distances sparking the ears of listeners who enjoy its pleasantry. The objective was to play in the path of passersby in order to receive donations but Bill had no doubt he could lure them like a snake as if his sax was a pungi.

That evening the famous religious leader Joyce Meyers appeared at the St. Louis Dome, Home of the Rams, to give a three-day presentation. Bill prepared for this, dressing very nicely with matching shirt and pants. His shoes were shined to a gloss and he wore a wide brim Levine cocked ace deuce on his head. he had two choices…work hard or work smart. He decided to work smart. He made his way over on the property near where people were waiting for the doors to open, instead of setting up across the street. As he played for the crowd a security officer stepped in front of him and demanded that he go across the street and "panhandle." Bill immediately stood up and addressed the officer. "Do I look like a panhandler?" The officer said no. "Then, don't insult my profession." Bill replied. The officer struck out his chest and told Bill "If you don't go across the street immediately I'll call the police department and have you arrested! You're disturbing the patrons!" The patrons were all just standing there, staring and listening. Bill didn't feel like dealing with the aggravation so he acquiesced and went across the street to play. The small crowd of patrons all came across the street and gave him a donation. All Bill could think was *Fairness should apply to all and not just some.* One of the patrons stated to Bill, "I can't believe he talked to you like that… we were all enjoying your music very much! I hope that you address the courts with this issue." They were right. Although the sidewalk was paved with bricks, Bill thought about the eight-inch perimeter owned by the city, where city lights were posted, which allowed him to play on other properties. He resolved to deal with the issue in the very near future and continued to play for his considerate fans. Despite the interference of security, it turned out to be a great day.

Bill's ability to survive depended on the donations he earned from playing music and some days were much better than others. Some days it would rain whereby he could not play until it stopped. Sometimes it did not stop, and on some rainy days one day led to another. These were the times when he knew the feeling of the *St. Louis Blues*. He could recall times of being so broke, that he couldn't *pay* attention. **Save Your Pennies for a Rainy Day** reflected more than mere words of a riddle. It was real life… a demanding reality.

Back at home, Bill began to review some of the scheduled events he planned to work, i.e. Cardinal's baseball, the Fox Theater, the Scottrade Center and The Pageant. He then opened the newspaper to look for any relevant upcoming events and happenings around the city that he could add to his schedule. Being a street musician had developed into a science of what to play, when to play and very importantly *where* to play. He used his personal knowledge of music and the city to determine which way to direct his flow.

Bill's place was very efficient, just enough for him, with five rooms: a kitchen, bedroom, bathroom, living room and an extra room where he set up his musical instruments, a computer and few pieces of equipment for recording music.   He also used that room to teach music. He called the room his studio. He spent a lot of time in the studio practicing, and writing his own original music. His most recent creation was a rap song that included the history of American Music:

Bump da bop-bop went the rhythm of the beat

As the angels up in heaven

Started to clap and stomp their feet

Jumping up and down with their halos in their hands

They turned the clouds of heaven to a hip-hop stage of dance

Knocking and a rocking until you'd thought it was a storm

As the music kept on flowing through that bebop hip-hop horn

The music reached down to the people

Under the simmering of the sun

And all God's children went to join in on the hip-hop fun

Even the devil came up from down under

And as he went towards the top He did a dance of hip-hop

Called the Pitchfork Hip-hop Drop

The rich and famous put their money on the shelf

As they went to the dance floor trying to find themselves

The hip-hop gangster rappers

Appeared at Club Seven and Eleven,

Rapping about the good life on the streets of hip-hop heaven

Trying to find the rhyme to send the sinners off and packing

But, you don't need a hook and line

When there's truth in what you're rapping

Oh Maybelline sang the guitar of the Rock in' roll man

As he rocked his famous duck walk

Into a Hip-hop dance of plan

For 50 years he's been rolling and raunchy

And rocking the country with music of merry

We wouldn't have that rock in' roll

If there wasn't a Chuck Berry

Michael Jackson was relaxing on white puffy clouds of sky

Although a man He still portrayed a child of shy

Billie Jean was on the hip-hop scene hoping he would stay

To her he was the one of all

But, he sang her the song Off The Wall

Because he didn't want to take the weight

She said "I am your baby's momma" and began to stalk

But, he stood and quickly disappeared

With the hip-hop moon of walk

Then the music went to the other side

Waking great spirits from their sleep

There was Beethoven composing a symphony

On timpani with the hip-hop beat

And let us not be forgotten of the great life of Scott Joplin

Who made dragged and hurry the cheerful of merry

His piano of concertinas brought moments of laughter

As we heard from the vines the sweet music of wine

As the hip-hop of love drops within us

And like the blue of gloom at midnight noon

On a ship at sea of silvery silhouette a flow

Like a Dixie tune under New Orleans moon

We hear the Saints hip-hopping in with 'Satchmo'

The Duke of Ellington spoke in Latin

To the hip-hopping Doll of Satin

And Ella Fitzgerald in a give it a whirl

Of scatting hip-hop refrains

They reached the bright of stardom

Through the heavenly gates of Harlem

On a hip-hop of thrill Locomotion of wheel

On Take the 'A' Train

And Ding went the bells of the chime

As we Count with the Basie of time

His finger snapping and tapping of shoes

Turned swing into hip-hop blues

That makes us leave all our troubles behind

Just as sure as the sun is of shine and Billie began to wake

To Good Mornings of Heartache

And Holidays of Weird Nightmares

And don't explain the blues as sax man Lester Young

Blew happily a hip-hop of song while the white flower

Lay of Lady Day let Ms. Brown to You sing the blues

And the trumpet of Dizzy and the sax of Bird

Were chopping out a rhythm people never had heard

Of razzle and dazzle and of spidlely do

Of sizzle and sazzle of hippity-hop and be-boppin' bop

We find the jubilee of rejoice in the smooth, romantic voice

In Moody's Mood for hip-hop love as King Pleasure sang

And the fun of chasing down the Giant Steps of

Hip-hop sound in a story told Of John Cole

Hip-hopping on the Trane

And the Man with the Golden Horn

Muted with echoing sounds of hip-hop music

And Milestones of Summer Time smiles

For Miles and Miles and Miles

And the Beatles sang I Want To Hold Your Hand

As the angels shook their heads and screamed

As they sailed the blue of sky in a Yellow Submarine

Singing merrily, merrily here in the heavenly

Life is a hip-hop dream

Then, the angels bowed their heads in devotion

When the mighty clouds of heaven stormed with distortion

As Jimmy Hendrix played the National Anthem

With a band of Gypsy men

His left hand would turn around

As he hip-hopped with his guitar upside down

And Janis Joplin and Bobby McGee

Sang with songs of glee while rocking to the hip-hop beat

Of her Mercedes Benz…And Johnny went to Cash in his dollars

As country fans hip-hopped and hollered

And Elvis Presley became a famous hip-hop rock star

Like a genius of the wiz

He brought to heaven the show of biz'

As he wiggled his hips and played his guitar.

And sometimes we had to wonder if Tupac stilled lived on

As we could still hear the echo of his voice in new of songs

But, he joins us now with hip-hop style

In heaven's clouds of cover

He wears the crown of 'King of Rap'

And still raps to his mother

And Marvin Gaye knew What Was Going On

As we listened to the hip-hop words of his songs

The thrill that we be feeling with Sexual Healing and

29

Ain't nothing like the Real Thing, So Let's Get It On

But, now that he has gone to rest

Hip-hopping on the climb of heavens steps

He sings Mercy, Mercy Me Hip hop ain't what it used to be

And Otis Redding had his day

Hip hopping on the dock of the bay

As his woman wore that same old shaggy dress

And as the cold of water grew of steep

And swelled up to his hip-hop feet

With ocean waves that cried out deep, Try A Little Tenderness

And like the ding in ring, B.B. King who

Made the hip-hop strings of Lucille sing

As muddy as the water of the blues

And the toe tapping sound of James Brown

Laid the hip-hop funk of rhythm down

While dancing in his patent leather shoes

And like a story told with a crown of gold

We cannot hop the hip Queen of Soul

All Aretha Franklin wants is some respect

And like a day in need of quench of thirst

We found Ray Charles in heaven's church

As he rectified and sanctified the Rumbling hip-hop set

The sun and the moon became birds of a feather

As they gravitated to the west

And hip-hopped from the east together

Gravity became a hip-hop music rhythm

As people joined hands throughout the universalism

And the stars in line and the lights at night of twilight time

In the sky above all came together

In a brighter glow of hip-hop love

The whole of galaxy was bumping up a beep of the bop

Now maybe you can understand why

They call it hip-hop!

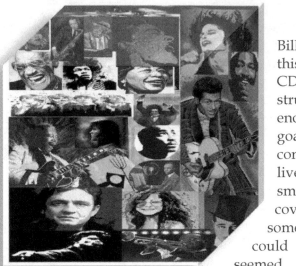

Bill hoped to one-day get this song recorded into a CD. However, he was a struggling artist. Having enough money to pursue his goals was a problem he constantly dealt with. He lived alone and with his small amount of earnings to cover his bills was sometimes more than he could handle. But, music seemed to always bring him through the hardest of times. Like most struggling artists, he had hopes of overcoming his hard times and making it big. He felt that only through his own actions of achievement could he accomplish this, but ultimately he knew it all rested in the hands of fate and being at the right place at the right time.

There was a sudden knock on the door. He quickly got up and slipped into his robe. It was Christy, a young woman who lived down the hall. "Hey Music Man!" she greeted. This was a name that people in the downtown area had come to call Bill. She wanted to borrow some money until her upcoming payday. She always promised to pay back on payday when she borrowed, but very seldom did. It sort of reminded Bill of the character of Wimpy in the cartoons of Popeye who would always ask for hamburgers with a promise to pay back on Tuesday. Inside he smiled. Bill did not mind. She invited him to many home cooked meals with her young daughter. As the saying goes, '*the way to a man's heart is through his stomach*', and he graciously accepted her offers to dine with her and her child knowing that this may be her way of paying back the money she couldn't really afford to give back to him. She was a good mother who made an honest living. Most importantly she was a decent person. That's what mattered in life to Bill. He stepped back into his apartment and took some bills from his black pouch while Christy waited in the hallway. He quickly returned and handed her $20.00. She thanked him, mumbled something about being late for work and was gone.

Bill tidied up his apartment and began to get ready to head downtown for the lunch hour where he normally began his day. Today, he would play his saxophone on the corner of 10th Street and Washington Avenue. He made it a practice to alternate his corner spots downtown. He thought it was good for business. He had several corners he alternately played during the lunch hour. Sometimes, he played for the late afternoon crowd getting off from work. He had to be creative when there were not many events going on in the city. He would find a spot where many people tended to walk by. Music was a very positive attraction and his line of work was definitely a self-contained business of public entertainment. He was, by all means, a public servant.

Chapter 5

I SAW YOU BUT
YOU DIDN'T SEE ME

Marlys was driving eastward bound on Washington Avenue in her customized, drop top, pink Mercedes, dressed up like a sophisticated lady. She wore her dangling, golden earrings with white pearls, and a diamond stone on her cute nose. Her lips were painted a tangerine, wet color. She wore a flimsy yellow, short skirt suit. Her head was wrapped with colorful nylon scarves to hide her distinguishably well-known dazzling crown of hair. It was an easy give-a-way. She stopped at the red light on Tucker Street. Pedestrians were standing on the corners waiting for the stoplight to change. There were many people walking along the sidewalks and passing in front of her car as they crossed to the other side of the street. She was focused on her destination, yet she became inspired while listening to an instrumental song on a satellite radio station she had tuned up in her car. She began to put lyrics to it that fit the picturesque scene like a stand-still of moment and time:

THE GREENLIGHTS OF LOVE

On the streets you will see people
Riding by in their cars
Riding low and riding high
Some are even riding towards the stars
The traffic lights shining bright
Let them know when to stop and go
Only if the crossroads to true love
Were so easy to unfold
The yellow lights would warn you to take caution on love's
highway... And when the red lights flash -- stop your love
or collide with heartbreak. But, when you see those green
lights of love-- Accelerate your heart don't let love slip
away! When those green lights of love shine on you, go for
it!
People are walking, standing and
Waiting for the stoplights to change
Speeding cars are coming from
Both directions trying to avoid an accident
Cause accidents are just like collisions...
But the stoplights won't lead them astray!
Only if the crossroads of love
Had stoplights to help them find their way
The yellow lights would warn you to take caution on
Love's highway... And when the red lights flash-- stop
Your love or collide with heartbreak... But, when you See
those green lights of love accelerate your heart Don't let
love slip away. When those
Green Lights of Love shine on you, go for it!

When the light turned green Marlys crossed into the intersection cruising at the speed of 20 miles per hour, slowing down to scout out a parking spot. She had an appointment with a producer from Los Angeles at the Renaissance Grand Hotel downtown. There was a garage, off site, associated with the hotel, a few feet from the hotel, but she preferred to park on the streets rather than parking in the garage. Yes, the garage may have provided on-camera protection, however, the streets provided more accessibility to her car, which was more important to her. The main downfall in parking on the streets though was the post event traffics jams that could be a pain in the butt, jigsaw puzzle getting out of.

She soon saw a parking space near the corner of 10th Street and Washington Avenue, in front of an elegant and busy restaurant and bar. She parked and began to immediately search her purse for change to put into the meter. Once out of her Mercedes and walking on the sidewalk, Marlys paused at the intersection waiting for a green light to walk. She noticed a man ahead dressed in black with his back facing her. She watched him as he began unfastening a case that was clutched in his arm. He also had a small, black chair that he was carrying which he unfolded and sat down on. When the traffic light turned green Marlys quickly crossed the street, walked a few feet from the corner and entered the entrance of the Renaissance Hotel.

Bill decided to stay close to home and head downtown rather than going west to the loop. He initially opted to set up near the corner of 10th Street and Washington Avenue, but he noticed that the area and the restaurant he would be playing near reflected a gloomy and dark shadow of emptiness. There was no one inside. Bill saw a sign on the steps leading to the front entrance: CLOSED FOR REPAIR UNTIL FRIDAY. Bill shrugged, gathered his things and then made his way to a different spot on 7th Street and Olive in front of Kinkos.

After her meeting, Marlys went shopping at her favorite retail establishment downtown on Olive, the Fur and Leather Gallery. She was excited about how well things went between her and the producer that she felt like rewarding herself with something nice. She had recently seen an outfit in the store that she had been eyeing. She searched through the racks of clothing until she found her size and then headed to the dressing room to try it on. The saleswoman inside the gallery offered assistance and let her into the dressing room. "That's a show stopping outfit you're trying on there. Come out and let me see how well you're wearing it!" Marlys nodded in agreement and hurried into the pink and compact dressing room. Soon she found herself unclothed and standing in front of a three-way mirror reflection of her nakedness. She was so ready to try on this mink and leather outfit. It was white silk on soft white leather outlined with mink trimmings with a gorgeously crafted embroidered design on the back. The jacket fit perfectly. While slipping into the bottom half of the ensemble, for an instant she thought she heard live music coming from a distance, but concluded that it must be the background music in the store. There was such a pleasant atmosphere in the gallery, and it smelled like a walk through the Botanical Gardens. A clear and refreshing perfumed fragrance of exotic flowers misted the air.

Meanwhile, the downtown traffic outside was light and only a few people ventured up and down the sidewalks. The afternoon rush hour had not yet begun. This was good for Bill because sometimes he arrived late and would miss a great portion of the lunch hour traffic. He took out his saxophone, but before he started to play, a man walked up to him and said, "Cues me Sir, can you spare a dollar so I can catch the bus?" Bill told the man that if you say "**excuse me**" I will give you a dollar. The man then pronounced excuse me very clearly. Bill gave him a dollar. The man thanked him, then turned around and left.

Bill began his afternoon of music playing songs of patriotism. He started with the *Star Spangled Banner*. Groups of people began crossing the intersection right into his path. They were headed north, south, east and west complimenting him with donations. A young woman with a very warm smile, dressed in bright colors, stopped and talked with him for a moment. She said, "Hi! Today is my mother's birthday and I was wondering if you could PLEASE play the *Happy Birthday* song for her." Since the lady was by herself he immediately wondered why she asked him to play. He smiled and said "Sure!", as he looked around for any sight of a possible mom type nearby. The lady enthusiastically pulled out her cell phone from her handbag and informed him that she was going to Skype her mom in on the moment. and began dialing a phone number. She spoke very briefly into the receiver and then turned to him. "Ok," she smiled with excitement, "Play the song!" She held the phone in the direction that captured Bill doing what he does best. Bill could actually see the lady's mother grinning as she waited for something to happen, and then he played the song with sensational liveliness. Bill could see the mother's face blossom into a bright smile, like the half moon that appears in the night sky. Her expression of happiness gave him a feeling of wholeness. The young woman thanked him again with a vigorous handshake and a generous donation.

A car suddenly pulled up and called to Bill with a beaconing finger. He walked over to the car and was passed a donation through a dark, tinted window. The person inside requested a *Duke Ellington* song called *Satin Doll*. Bill happily played it while he danced back to his spot on the sidewalk. He loved to play nostalgic songs of the past, music that contributed to the culture of America, and the public seemed to recognize and enjoy this style of music.

There was a shabbily dressed woman walking slowly down the street coming towards Bill holding a bag in her arms. Bill spoke to her as she passed by. "How are you feeling today?"   She stopped for a moment and said that she was having a bad day. She asked Bill if he was making any money. Bill said yes. She then asked him if he could spare a dollar to help her get something to eat. Bill recalled seeing the woman downtown several times before pan-handling the passersby and figured that she was homeless. He reached into his duffel bag and handed her two dollars and some change. She thanked him and walked off. "God bless her," he said to himself. He could relate to the conditions of destitution, for he had been homeless before and living on the streets, also. Whether or not she was going to get something to eat with the money was irrelevant. This did not differentiate her need for help, which is what really mattered. As long as he had done the right thing, what the other person did was on them.

Back at the Fur and Leather Gallery, Marlys exited the store clutching a package in her arms and began walking east on Olive Street, turning at the corner of 7Th Street. She passed by a group of men dressed in typical business attire walking in the opposite direction. They whistled and echoed *cat calls* as they passed her. One of them yelled, "You look good babe!" Her body made you do them kinds of things. She turned and gave them a polite smile as she continued to parade down the sidewalk.

She could clearly hear music coming from a near distance. She saw a man sitting in a small chair playing the saxophone, the same man she had seen earlier on 10Th Street and Washington Avenue. She thought, "Wow, he sounds good!" As she got closer she looked into his clean-shaved face and brown, compassionate eyes and realized that he was the musician she had met on The Riverfront. An instant smile of delight came to her face. She stood in front of him for a moment and just listened, but he didn't appear to notice her. She wasn't going to interrupt him. She reached into her purse and removed some bills, crumpled them together and placed them into his duffel bag, then hurried to her car.

Bill was playing hard and passionately, but he could always sense when money was being dropped into his bag. He looked up instinctively as he encountered a faint, subtle, sweet and enticing fragrance of perfume that filled his sense of smell with a pleasant, tingling sensation. He could see a woman walking away from him. She had the most beautiful and sexy shaped legs, and her hips were packed like a shotgun, thick and tightly fitted into a very short, yellow skirt with a hem well above her silk stocking thighs. Her bottom was loaded and it swished from side to side like two healthy sacks of flower. It bounced up and down like a rubber ball as she danced down the street to the rhythm of Bill's hip-hop saxophone beat. She had an alluring way of walking with the steady groove of a *Count Basie* swing. "What a beautiful behind," Bill said out loud. The small crowd of listening fans all turned to look. "Where EVER she's going I sure would like to ride her all over town." He started to hear the chorus of a hit made famous by Ray Charles, Shake A Tail Feather, in his head, '...can I see you bend over and let me see you shake a tail feather!' The crowd moved along as Bill started to make his horn sing the same song. "If only I could have seen her face," he thought. He imagined that she was as beautiful as the sweetest breath of song. He began to compose something creative and bluesy and new right there on the spot...

I Used To Ride My Baby

I used to ride my babe, all over town
I said, I use to ride my babe all over town
There ain't no other girl like her around!

You know my babe's like a car with a big trunk
I said, my babe's like a car with a big trunk
Tight skirts on her hips and
headlights in the front!

I'd ride her until you'd hear squeaks in her
seats
Oh, I'd ride her 'til you'd hear
squeaks in her seats
I'd drive her so fast until her tires
would screech!

One day I mashed her gear down to the floor
My Babe started to roll, but she wouldn't roar
Her knees began to knock down to her feet
Her radiator started to over heat
But, when she began to steam and her
Motor started to thump
I said to myself it must be her Water pump!

I used to ride my babe, all over town
I said, I use to ride my babe, all over town
Can't ride no more since her
Water pump broke down!

Bill turned his attention back to the downtown streets and played the song *I Love You Just the Way Are.* As he looked towards the flow of traffic he noticed the most beautiful, pink, drop top directly in front of him with pink wall tires and golden spinning rims. The woman driving the car slowed down, and to Bill's surprise, blew him a kiss from the palm of her hand, then waved and quickly sped off. Bill blushed. An instant glimpse of her resembled the Princess that he had met on The Riverfront, but he quickly dismissed it as a silly thought and decided *It was Just My Imagination, once again, running away with me.*

Chapter 6

IT JUST AIN'T FAIR

It was a Tuesday afternoon as Bill sat on the corner of 7th Street and Pine Street playing his saxophone. He began to feel the showering heat of the hot summer sun blazing on his uncovered forehead. Hot weather around the city seemed to be very consistent. However, the winter days were unpredictable and wishy-washy. It could be raining on one side of the street and not on the other; heavily snowing one day and the sun brightly shining the next. The city has been known to experience four seasons in one day! They say, *If you don't like the weather wait about ten minutes and it will change.*

He began to reminisce back to the wonderful time of last year's Christmas when he played on the streets of Grand Avenue for the patrons of the Fox Theater as people attended the season's finale of entertainment. This section of Grand was referred to as *The Intersection of Art and Life/Grand Center.* A few feet away from the Fox stood the Cranzberg Arts Center. Close by was the Black Repertoire Theater. The Scott Joplin Museum was also located near the area. Sitting on the corner of Grand Boulevard and Washington Avenue stood the Third Baptist Church. He played his saxophone directly across the street from the main entrance of the Fox Theater where he could also caught the crowd from the Paul Symphony Hall, The Jazz Bistro, The Kota Bar and Restaurant, The Sheldon Concert Hall and The Best Steak House as people walked to and from the lots of parking spaces along the back streets. A short distance from where he played was a statue of Leon R. Strauss, an Urban Pioneer and Preservationist of St. Louis. His accomplishment includes the restoration of the Fabulous Fox Theater, which has contributed to the heritage of St. Louis for many years.

At the onset of winter Christmas Carols rang out from the bell of Bill's saxophone as it would echo with joy up and down Grand Boulevard. The cheerful holiday melodies heard once a year brought bright moments to the faces of the listeners. Bill also thought of Christmas as a special time for musicians as well, as they heightened the season's spirit with song. But, it wasn't Christmas Season. If his song choice is centered around playing songs of the season, then it was absolutely, positively time to ring out Gershwin's *Summertime!*

Across the street from where Bill played, there was a woman dressed in a gown like garment sitting on the bench at a bus stop. On her lap was a stack of magazines and newspapers. She threw each magazine and newspaper on to the pavement after swiftly thumbing through the pages. There was something in one of the magazines that brought a smile to her face revealing a mouth filled with gold teeth, which is typically Black St. Louis. Soon, there was trash strewn all around her. She had created a total mess. The bus arrived; the woman boarded it and was gone. Bill thought to himself how disgusting this was. He walked across the street, picked up the trash and placed it in a nearby trash receptor sitting beside the bus stop. But, before he went any further to criticize the woman's behavior he gave the situation more meaningful thought. He had observed the destination of the bus she boarded and concluded that she was from the North Side where there are no public trash receptors. There are a few here and there that proprietors and residents had placed in front of their businesses and homes. Her behavior was typically learned from the lack of public neighborhood trash receptors. 'Just throw the trash onto the streets', is the behavior that many North Side residents have come to adopt in response to the inadequate community accommodations. *Fairness should apply to all and not just some.* This incident made Bill think more about Grand Avenue. There are always good things and bad things about a person place or thing, and in Bill's humble opinion, the nastiest of all his travels on the public transit system was when he got off at the Grand.

43

THE GRAND

Have you ridden on the Grand Blvd Metrolink Elevator
lately?
It doesn't matter if it's been sooner; the odor it carries is
always the same
I'm not talking about the delicious
Smell of put n' tang
Or the scent of peppermint from a sweet candy cane
But the stringent odor of urine that permeates the nostrils
of your nose
And soils the fresh fragrance of your clothes
Don't lean against the walls
And cautiously touch the buttons
That takes you up or down,
For they are often covered with sticky grime of many
shades and kinds
And when you exit make sure you wipe the bottom
Of your tennis sneaker tees so that you won't track a
disease
Onto the train or overcrowded bus, or even the front room
floor
Where you live, possibly giving an illness
To your household or to your friends
Who may have never been in the Grand Blvd Metrolink
Elevator

Don't risk being a carrier!
Take the steps!

Very often the elevator doesn't work anyway
But when it does and you step into it there's
Nothing left to be said
The Missouri Board of Commission for Health
Needs to quit turning its head

There are options of shutting it down or
Installing portable restrooms
Cleaning it doesn't seem to work[5]

We, the passengers of the Metro Link Transit System
Are not peons or jerks!
Yet, you want to raise the transit system fare
Wave you hands in the air like you just don't care!
Threatening us with lock up for eating on the train
Or drinking from a cup
Solving other problems to keep the transit systems fat
But this is one problem you need to do more than look at...

FIX THAT!

---

[5] The Grand Metro Link has recently been remodeled, but without the convenience of restrooms.

Bill began to notice the traffic becoming very thin and then suddenly there was commotion in the streets. Red and blue lights began to flash along with the beeping of a siren. Police cars blocked the intersection as three men exited a late model, blue car and began to run off. The police officers followed them in hot pursuit. They were headed towards Bill. One of the men ran so fast until he tripped over Bill's duffel bag spilling some of the money from the bag out into the streets. Bill hurried to pick it up as the fallen criminal, unyieldingly, got back up. Finally a police officer finally caught up and apprehended the assailant, handcuffing him from behind and forcing him back to the ground. The other two assailants disappeared into the crowd of people as the remaining officers continued the chase. Everyone stood along the streets watching in shock. This disruption clearly brought an abrupt end to the lunch hour of music entertainment.

A bystander yelled out vehemently, "Why don't they take those kinds of people and put them all together so they can rob and steal from each other!" Bill thought to himself that this concept was already a reality; Government Housing Projects are being built throughout the city at a tremendously rapid pace. The purpose of the Projects is to provide housing for low-income people. However, the majority of the Housing Project residents are poor Black people. An overwhelmingly large percentage of these Black faces peer through the gloomy bars and dirty windows of the prisons, the City Jail and the Work House. They have no resources to obtain a private attorney for their defense and money to make bail. For many of them their gruesome judicial destination is systematically determined from the moment of their arrest. They are intelligent human beings, the same as you and I. However, they may not necessarily be smart because their hustle is wrong. But, on all *four corners* the standard rule is if you don't have a job you need to have a hustle because your hand is the hand that will feed you. And if you were hungry what would you do? Gambling with their life and going against the odds of fate is the only life they've ever known. They fail to devise a viable plan, like *an education*,[6] to help them escape the poverty of the Hood. Instead, they come up with a scheme, and schemes only lead to trouble. Many of them are incarcerated for drug related offenses. For

---

[6] Young women in Nigeria and Afghanistan are risking their lives for an education and for their rights to one and here in America people pass by schools every day and won't even take the time to go IN and get a GED!

various lengths of time, these low lives and hood rats, thugs, criminals and societal deviates have been penalized for their transgressions by being taken from the streets and placed behind bars to prevent them from continuing unlawful activities, and causing destruction in people's lives and creating endless havoc. The irony of this situation is that these Black people don't own planes, nor do they own sail boats, which are the resources for bringing drugs into our country and targeting the Black Communities. The great *Sam Cook* testified with a song **titled *A Change Is Gonna' Come...*** It seems like waiting for a change is the same as waiting for *Gabriel* to blow his trumpet. *GOD* created the earth and there's nothing here that belongs to the devil. It's the human abuse of what *GOD* created that makes it evil.

There are many who remember the notorious Pruitt Igoe Projects that stood in the area of Jefferson Avenue and Cass Avenue. Black people were stacked on top of each other floor after floor like potato sacks. Crime infested every crevice of these Government Housing Projects on a magnificent scale breaking level. The *Terrifying Assassin* Earl Junior and his fierce predecessor Sam *'Street Justice'* Petty roamed these grounds flourishing crime and punishing their victims at will. This type of housing has a tendency to become a community within itself. The enforcement of proper laws and sometimes special laws may be what is needed to accommodate the environment. Concern of how people may come to live in this type of community of close proximity needs to have a higher priority. Now, the buildings have a more moderately town house styled construction, but the concept has not changed. It sounds like the insanity of repeating the same thing over and over, but each time expecting different results. Since we cannot turn to the builders to differentiate the outcome of these more sophisticatedly built Government Projects from the previous ones, let us turn to *GOD*.

The commonly used phase in the Black community, *"I can't be successful in society because I'm Black,"* is no longer altogether true. Some could argue that it is irrelevant. It's the old way of rationalizing one's behavior. This train of thought can alienate a person from being a positive member of society. Now, we have a Black President. Let me reiterate that, PRESIDENT BARACK OBAMA is a Black man! Maybe now there really is hope, because this is one of the most significant and greatest changes in United States History. President Obama has set the standards of achievements for the Black man very high. You *can* be what you want in this great country of America! Dr. Martin Luther King's dream is gradually coming to light. It has become a vivid reality. Today, it's not so much about Black and White, the race of the people; it's more about the class of modern society. Money has found a way to disrupt any society. It is the color of green and *GREEN* is really all that matters. Whatever it is that might be holding you back is based on the poor choices you make in your effort to get to where you want to be. For example, you say "*I'm go' play my radio, turn it up cause' it's too low!*" But, when you leave the Hood you best turn down your ghetto songs because you're driving through a red light into the wrong. Understandably, the nature of some people is to rebel against certain boundaries of rules and regulations as a reaction to the life conditions they have been subjected to. This behavior can easily be diagnosed as a medical condition of a *personality defensive defiance disorder.* However, for many, when adhering to the rules and guidelines of success that society has provided us *it's So Easy A Cave Man Can Do it...* so it seems.

A cab driver from the Middle East who often gave Bill courtesy rides in his Wilson's Cab once said to him, "What's wrong with the Black people in this city? They rob and steal from each other. They have no sense of brotherhood. They show no respect for one another, nor do they care about each other. They are so hung up on what the White man has done to them in the past until they let that issue interfere with their future and social obligations to be a part of mainstream society. They need to let it go." He went on to say, " Where ever they go, they take their negative behavior with them from the Hood and fail to conform." Bill began to feel a bit of resentment because he was Black people, but he quickly checked himself and kept his ears open to the valid information. He knew that the cab driver was referring to a particular class of Black people, which he probably dealt with on a regular basis in the tough streets of the city. While he agreed in some way with the cabby, Bill reflected on the times when he played music in other cities. People would ask him why are guys from St. Louis so cool? [7] [8]. His response to this was that you have to be from St. Louis to know that, in the same way as you have to be Black to fully understand the realities of a Black

---

[7] *Birth of the Cool*; by jazz trumpeter Miles Davis He was born in East St. Louis, Ill. Miles Davis has been hailed as the coolest man to have walked the planet.

[8] *The Jazz Singer*; by Eddy Jefferson

person, which the cab driver was not. "They are so dependent on the Government," the driver continued, "until they believe with resentment the fallacy that our progress as foreigners in this country is based on Government Assistance. They fail to comprehend that we as a people of unity brought progress with us when the Government afforded us the opportunity to make this country our home. "Now we have a Black President," he stated further. He turned around and looked at Bill as he continued. "But, I wonder if he can do it?" he said sincerely. Bill asked him, "Do what?" He looked Bill straight in the eye and said emphatically, "Introduce to legislation a law that will contribute pride to the BLACK AMERICANS."

Change is happening before our very eyes. Step out from the dark doorways, the dingy dilapidated homes and suburban communities. Raise your hand. *Lift Every Voice and Sing.* Music has no color or face. It touches every human being, every spirit of the world. Join hands with your brothers and sister, not just in church, but also in your daily lives. Be a part of it. Stand up and testify about the troubles in your life, the existing problems in our vast society. We can make it happen. Bring it to the streets. Break the barriers that have been set around your neighborhoods and around your life that keep you from reaching the potential of what you could become. Our plight needs to take flight like *'Charlie 'Bird' Parker* and soar our flail of wings into the air with the dazzling quickness of bebop rhythm, gliding through the sleet and rain like a freight *Chasin' The Trane* cause' *Now Is The Time* to break free from *Impressions* and voice your real expressions. "This is *The Street Musician* talking to you."

The streets of downtown St. Louis were crowded with people whispering, pointing and commenting on the criminal disruption. Bill overheard that the three men were being pursued for stealing a car. He watched as one was caught and put into a police car. The two that got away would be pursued tonight. They hung out at Lucas Park, known to the street people as Hobo Park. It sits across the street from the Larry Rice Shelter. Anyone sitting on a bench, hanging and begging on the streets, on a regular, was subject to end up in jail for complaints of loitering, public intoxication, peace disturbance, trespassing and panhandling. Many of the homeless already had warrants issued for failure to make court appearances for minor offenses. They only seemed to pursue small amounts of money to get by.

Although his earnings were meager, Bill considered himself very fortunate to have a talent that earned him an honest living. But, he felt kinship to the people who were less fortunate, hopeless, homeless and hungry. He could relate to those who had little and seemed contented with living simple lives. Perhaps their paths of lives were not by choice. He chose music as his path of life, but he was not satisfied with the typical and characteristic conditions of being a starving artist. He was driven to want more. He read papers, loved a good book and had a few magazines; he watched TV, DVDs and movies and he listened to music on CDs and on the radio, and he could hear his story being told, being heard, being watched. He believed that if he stayed true to his convictions of music, the joy and happiness it brought to people around the world, the hands of fate would eventually allow him a time of prosperity. A big part of being successful is not giving up.

He enjoyed being a *Street Musician,* but he did want to elevate his music to a higher level of performance. Music encompasses a vast, undefined power of affect on our lives. Bill thought of music as a blossoming flower of compassion onto a society of humanity, like the sweet scent of a bushel of roses into the mist of air where people took a deep breath of relief from the pressures of life. They enjoy, mingle, become human and share a love for one another. He wanted to blossom like a rose and so he continued to emphatically pursue his dream. He did not relish the joy of pain disappointment often brought. But, he believed there must be a rainbow somewhere in the middle of the road. He simply wanted to reach that rainbow. The human intellect can become very complicated with detail, however, wisdom is very simple. So is the beauty of music. Every man and woman should have a song in their heart. The rhythm of life can get a little funky sometimes.   But, don't give up on your dream. *Keep it real.* He gathered his duffel bag and slung it across his shoulder. He began to walk slowly down the street singing the lyrics of a favorite song.

IT ALL COMES BACK

IT ALL COMES BACK

Give a hand to someone with sad eyes
and fill them up with love
Then watch them bloom into happiness
You will find out it's true, it all comes back to you
Give a hand to a lover with a broken heart
And let them know, there's other broken hearts
That wants to make a new start
You will find out its true, it all comes back to you
There's not enough love going
Around in the world
To make a better place for everyone
But when your dreams go astray
Love will help you find away
To turn your dreams to real
If love is what you feel
And when your dreams come true
Give love to someone and
It will all come back to you

Chapter 7

THE MAKING OF A STAR

Marlys lay under the blazing heat of the sun in the backyard of her beautiful home. She relaxed thoughtfully in her pillowed lawn chair. Her voluptuous body was dressed in a bright, orange bikini bathing suit. She dipped her pedicured feet into the blue, cold water of the pool that stretched along the brick, castle like wall that enclosed her property, giving her complete seclusion from her neighbors. Marlys covered her face with a wide brim, straw hat as the sun beamed down from the sky onto her body. Her creamy, caramel skin glistened from a heavy coat of lemon scented sun tan lotion. This was her haven when she was not out and about, traveling, or performing.

A mother of three children, currently away at summer camp, Marlys reflected on how blessed she was. She had a young son and two very talented young daughters that wanted to be like their mother. The older of the two was a talented artist who spent much of her time perfecting her talent. She also played guitar. The youngest daughter played the saxophone. They were both taking private lessons of piano and dance.

Her home was extravagant and much too big for a single mother. Like most newly made stars, Marlys' talent allowed her to upgrade her life in any way she had ever dreamed. She always knew that if she made it, she would remember her family and friends. It was just her way. Many of them worked with for her in some capacity during her rise in the music industry. Her sister, Cindy, lived with her. She worked as an accountant the Hyatt Hotel located in downtown St. Louis. Cindy also worked for Marlys as an accountant. In addition to her household was a live-in maid that took care of cleaning, cooking, and other household duties.

Marlys had not always been so prosperous in her career of music. She had lived through some very difficult times in pursuit of her dreams, having three children to take care of. She worked various jobs that sometimes paid minimum wage, which often provided marginal living conditions. She could remember being unemployed, with no money, and so far behind in her rent until she was haunted with the threat of eviction and becoming homeless. But through sheer conviction and perseverance, music always came through to save her from the pitfalls of destitution.

She could vividly remember the struggles of starting her own band working in the local clubs around St. Louis. One particular incident forced her to make a decision on how to conduct her business affairs. She remembered an engagement she played at the Red Palace Night Club. The contract agreement was for her to play the club for the sum of $1000.00. Verbal contracts are typical for local musicians, which is what she made.

It was a Saturday night and the Red Palace Club was jumping with excitement. The doors of the club steady swung open all night long. There were wall-to-wall people. Gypsy and The Stars of Venus, which consisted of Marlys and two other gorgeously beautiful female vocalists had acquired a very large following throughout the city. The performance went exceptionally well and the fans loved them. However, at the show's end, the manager came up to Marlys and complained of a very strict budget and overhead. She paid them the sum of $500.00. Marlys looked at the sum of money confused and upset, but despite every effort of persuasion, she could not convince the manger to live up to their agreement. From that moment on, she never again entertained without being paid first. She demanded her payment up front before she began her show with a written and legally binding contractual agreement. This strict policy developed into an image that followed her, depicting her as a hard business woman. Eventually her music career began to grow and prosper, and her group became the best performing local group in the city, winning several awards. A while later they landed some recording time at the Jupiter Recording Studio. She had been persistently writing songs, and now she was able to have them recorded. She worked diligently at this project, guiding her group into a venture they would never forget, shaping their lives into a dream of a life time. Things began to pay off for big. Their CD was finally produced and played over local radio stations. Ultimately, they were offered an opportunity to perform in a local movie with their music as background throughout extent of the movie's production. *Gypsy and the*

Stars of Venus were legitimate local celebrities. Magazines and newspapers held them as the up and coming stars of St. Louis. They had finally made the big time, at least, in the world that they knew of.

The group soon scored an interview with the Capitol Recording Company. The interviewers raved on how much they loved their music. They talked to Marlys separately, as the leader of the group, and offered her a contract to become a national recording artist. There was a stipulation however, which brought about utter disappointment. The Recording Company only wanted Marlys. She was the creator of the songs, and the backbone of the group.[9] She talked it over with the other members, and they unanimous agreed that she should take the opportunity. It only comes around once in a life time, so go For It!

That very night they celebrated at the Tangerine Club. It was a gala of an affair. The next morning Marlys flew to The Big Apple, to a new life, a world of glamour, endless fun, great excitement, and hard work that paid off big. Her local CD soon evolved from a production of thousands in a production of millions. She took on the name *The Queen of Venus* and soon became a super hip-hop star.

---

[9] The trend of record companies choosing the star of the group and eliminating the other group members began in the late 1950's with artists such as Frankie Lymon and The Teenagers and in the 60's with the Queen of Rock N' Roll, Janis Joplin.

Chapter 8

A NEW FOUND FRIEND

The Busch Stadium was filled with excitement as the St. Louis Cardinals were set to play against the New York Giants. The streets were filled with bumper-to-bumper cars. Flashing red lights and traffic safety patrol officers were scattered about. Guys were yelling, "Tickets for sale." People were selling colorful beads. Stands were selling Cardinal baseball caps and T shirts along with souvenirs and trinkets, ice cold bottled water, peanuts and cracker jacks. People walked in streams along the streets headed towards the Stadium. Musicians stood along the busy sidewalks playing their instruments. The noise was overwhelming.

Bill sat at the corner of 8th Street and Clark Street under the stairs that led to the Stadium's parking lot. Fireworks were set off every time the Cardinals scored a run followed by an uproar that filled the atmosphere. After a couple of hours had passed people began to trickle out of the Stadium. Bill began to play on his saxophone the song *What's Going On* by Marvin Gaye. The massive crowd was soon coming from the stadium. They were happy. The Cardinals had defeated the New York Giants!

"Play that horn, man!" someone yelled. The crowd was exuberant with excitement as the saxophone belched out the tune *Take Me out to the Ball Game* and a long list of many more. As the progression of traffic continued, Bill stood up and played the song *America*. An ocean of red continued to flood out of the Stadium and onto the cross streets for block after block.

The crowd began to fizzle as Bill played beautiful ballads. The tone of his saxophone filled the air with a sweet, penetrating sound. It was peaceful. The streets were practically deserted. He sat down taking his instrument apart. He gathered his duffel bag and removed the donations. It was 11:30 P.M. His thoughts were of heading home and calling it a day. He began to pack his saxophone into the duffel bag. There was a shadow blocking the light. He looked up suddenly. There was someone standing over him, a tall man wearing a blue uniform with emblems and a silver badge attached to his short sleeve shirt. He was a police officer.

"Man, you sound good! Where did you learn to play the sax like that? You should be on the inside of the Stadium!" Before Bill could respond, the stranger continued. "Oh, excuse me, I hope I'm not interrupting you, but my name is Tommy. I work for the St. Louis Police Department, in the Traffic Division. I direct the traffic for most of the baseball games and I hear you playing your saxophone all the time. When I'm not here, I direct the traffic at the Scottrade Center and I hear you playing there, also." Bill stood up and shook the strangers extended hand. "I've been playing for a lot of years," he said. "I had some schooling along the way." "It sounds like you've been around," the man said. Bill introduced himself and said, "What's the Cardinal's next move?" "They're going to play in Houston next week and then they're going to Milwaukee," Tommy replied. "That was the best version of *America* I've heard!" Bill was not very responsive to compliments. In fact, he was rather shy when he was not playing his saxophone. But, he accepted the compliment with a thank you.

Bill began to walk with giant steps to catch the train to the American Center on Washington Avenue. From there, he could easily walk home. He grabbed his duffel bag, slung it over his shoulder, and then headed across the street towards the Stadium's Metro Train Terminal. There were many red T-shirts and caps as Cardinal fans were waiting to board. The train was crowded, but Bill managed to find a seat. He exhaled a deep breath when he sat down as the train scurried down the track. He closed his eyes and dosed for a moment, but when he opened them again, the train was crossing the Mississippi River into East St. Louis, Illinois. He jumped up alarmingly. He had missed his stop. Fortunately, the train had not traveled far. The next stop was at the Casino Queen Gambling Boat. He got off there to board the next train going back to St. Louis.

As he sat on the opposite side of the tracks waiting, he took out his saxophone and began to play. He knew many songs that portrayed the essence of human emotion, but the feeling of the blues reflected in most of the music he played. He began to blow the heartfelt spirit of the blues.

He boarded the train with his saxophone still attached to the strap around his neck, and the passengers turned to look with an expression of wonder and excitement. Someone yelled from the back, "Are you going to blow that thing for us, dog?" As he sat down, a famous song by the Great Duke Ellington came to mind. He began to play *Take the A Train*. A young lady sitting across the aisle from him said, "What else do you play?" He said, "I play the blues," and placed his duffel bag into the isle. People began getting up and dropping donations in it. As the train neared St. Louis, he could see the illuminating network of lights on the riverbank. He thought about his city, St. Louis being 'The Home of Rhythm & Blues'[10] and he made his saxophone sing the blues with a dancing tempo and a bouncing rhythm. The passengers began to clap their hands giving him a rhythmic beat. The train was rock 'n rolling, like Chuck Berry, across the great river.

---

[10] *Autobiography* by W.C. Handy: The blues was brought to St. Louis Missouri by trumpeter W.C. Handy during the turn of the 19th Century, whereby St. Louis earned the reputation as The Home of Rhythm & Blues. Today rhythm and blues is the featured entertainment in the community of Soulard located in South St. Louis.

THE DIRTY ST. LOUIS BLUES

The Blues has been around since
there was water in the sea
You know, the blues has been around since
there was water in the sea
The blues is in the air and it preys on you and me

You know, I'll play some rock n' roll
when I want to sooth my soul
I said I'll play some rock n' roll
when I want to sooth my soul
But, when I get bad news there's nothing like
The Dirty St. Louis Blues

I've had the Dirty St. Louis Blues for a long, long time
I said, I've had The Dirty St. Louis Blues
for a long, long time
Messing with The Dirty St. Louis Blues
I almost lost my St. Louis mind

You know, my momma had The Dirty St. Louis Blues
And my daddy had it, too
I said, my momma had The Dirty St. Louis Blues
And my daddy had it, too
Seems like The Dirty St. Louis Blues
Is passed around Like we pass around the flu

You know, my sister tried to have a different life
She wore diamonds and furs
I said, my sister tried to have a different life
She wore diamonds and furs
She thought she couldn't catch them Dirty Blues
But, they shoul' caught up with her

I got the St. Louis Blues…I got
The Dirty, dirty blues
I got the St. Louis Blues…I got
The Dirty, dirty blues
I got the St. Louis Blues…I got
The Dirty, Dirty blues

Nelly's style of rap make your fingers start to snap
And you can feel his Country Grammar to your shoes
And Chuck Berry was in a hurry
to let his music make you merry
With that groovy rock n' roll rhythm, too
Charlie Parker called it be-bop
And now the people call it hip-hop
But, all of them are talking about
The Dirty St. Louis Blues

You might have money in the U.S. Bank
And wear New York alligator shoes
You might have money in the U.S. Bank
And wear New York alligator shoes
But, just as sure as one and one makes two
The Dirty St. Louis Blues
Is gonna catch up with you!

The train entered the Riverfront Terminal. It pulled up to the platform at a leisurely fashion. Bill had gained a second wind. He quickly exited the train, went down the flight of stairs, and began to walk up 2nd Street. This section of the Riverfront was called Laclede's Landing meticulously carved with brick and stone buildings reserved from the late 1800's.

Chapter 9

LACLEDE'S LANDING

The bars and clubs were packed and spilled patrons onto the cobble stone streets, which were filled with tourists, college students, drunken business men, couples, friends, strangers, the wondering homeless and hustlers, beggars, cars, cabs, and horse driven carriages touring passengers around the historic scenery.

Bill looked at his cell phone to check the time. It was 11:45PM. He normally didn't play his saxophone on the Landing until after midnight. He passed by the Wax Museum and looked through the window. There were life size dolls of Superman, Dracula, a figure that resembled the Devil, Batman, and The Black Magic Woman. Bill began to imagine himself as a life size doll behind the window of the Wax Museum holding his saxophone. He would call himself Mister B.

MISTER B TO THE RESCUE

Up

Down

Back and forth

Went many pretty girls

Mister B would whirl and twirl them

On a trip around the world

With his pied piper pipe of silver and gold

Blowing tells of stories that have been untold

They danced with fun as if hypnotized

Some grooved to the rhythm and were mesmerized

Mister B

Took a deep breath

And tried to figure out the plot

He was burning with sensation

From foot of bottom to the head of top

Even the Devil climbed through a manhole

And came up to the top for a breath of cool air 'cause hell was too hot

He wore a Gothic red shirt from

His shoulders to his hips

And carried a long black pitchfork

That sizzled with flaming fire at the tip

He had a Gothic bible in his hand

For he was a religious man

He went to church on Sundays

And Saturdays as well

In his other hand he had a leather zip lock bag

To carry sinful souls with him on

His trip back to hell

The Black Magic Woman

Came onto the Landing scene

Entertaining with love and devotion,

And serving spells of potions of lotion

From a magic love machine

She had the Presley charisma of

Rock n' roll Elvis

And wore a short black skirt that

Stopped at her pelvis

Her face was sweetly cute like Hanna Montana

As she told the tell of the famous voodoo spell she whipped
on Carlos Santana

Dracula came out in a silk black cape

And long white fangs with

Golden and diamond caps

And a tilted black Levine with a wide brim

His nocturnal pimping topped

The legacy of Pimping Iceberg Slim

He wore Tommy Hilfiger designer

Black leather jeans

Which were encased with white pearls

And red ruby studs

He was on a mission with vampire intentions to taste in his venomous mouth

The dripping red-hot thick of pretty girls' blood

Mighty Mouse was on his way to save the day

And get the situation well in hand

But he wouldn't show his face

On the Landing place

Because the Pink Panther and Felix the Cat

Knew about his plan

Superman took a flight from high in the sky

And tried to stop the evil plight

Of this horror filled night

But the dogs of sin stepped in with a grin

Like rin tin tin and fed him kryptonite

Then Batman drove through the Landing

In his bat mobile ride

With silver spinning spoke of wheels

That treaded the cobble stone streets

With an easy glide

But as he moved from his car of black leather seat

He was overpowered and met up with defeat

For his days of being strong were long gone without Robin
by his side

Mister B stepped in with his bling bling

Of silver medallion cross and spirit of golden horn

And rid the scene of evil deeds

Until the night was done

The Devil stood with a pout on his face,

But had nothing left to say

He grimaced for a while then threw in the tile

And quietly went away

The Black Magic Woman dabbed her body portions with
potions of love lotion

Then blew Mister B a wet red kiss that didn't miss

But smacked his lips as he dipped

To his hips and fell

Now he was haunted with the notion

That the kiss held a potion

To cast him under a voodoo spell

After a while the silver moon looked down with a bright half smile

As if giving it's safe of consent

Like a video recorder it captured the order of the whole outlandish event

Soon the Landing town was safe and sound

As far as eyes could see

Thanks to the man with the plan to blow his horn

The Street Musician

Mister B

The Landing Crew

Pretty girls wore wrap around
And open top blouses
And silk lace shirts
Some wore tightly fitted
Swaying hips
See-thru miniskirts some wore heels
And dressed in chic
Some barefooted tipsy
On the cobble stone bricks
Some were skinny....some were fat
some were walkie-talkie willow
Pretty prancing pussycats
Some were sweet as juicy chewy tootsie
Like Beyonce's sugar pie cuties
Bending over and jingling their booty.
Some were short and some were tall
Some didn't wear black panty hose
Or white cotton draws.
A delicious picture sight to see of scene
Like having lunch at burger king
Hot cross buns with shredded cheese
Marinated in sauce
And double burger between.

Bill sat on the corner of 2nd Street and Morgan Street. A tower clock stood a short distance from him and a huge parking lot was behind him. The Wax Museum was a diagonally across from him. The Morgan Street Brewery was cater-corner, and on the 4th corner was GIGGERS Bar and Restaurant. A barbecue stand stood in front of the club filling the air with an aroma of good taste.

Playing music on the streets every day, Bill saw some of the same familiar faces where ever he played. He recognized a few of the street people hanging along the dimly lit corners and pathways dubiously asking for donations to the homeless, or trying to engage people in the famous con game of three card molly. Some were just outright begging. It was all a trick to swindle innocent people out of their money, who were out and about on the Landing to merely have a good time. One of the street people spoke to Bill with all the attitude of the street that they could naturally muster, a fellow that goes by the name of Whoopee Do.

"Bill The Music Man! Who do you think you are; A late bloomer, like Denzel Washington?"
Bill smirked while shaking his head. "You can just call me Dollar Bill, Whoopee Do."
"I've never worked and never will! People work for the Dollar Bill."
"Well," Bill smiled and said, "Just shake my hand now Whoopee Do, because it's going to cost you money to shake it later." The hard humor

caused them to burst into laughter as they smacked hands together with a knuckle-pulling grip of handshake.

"I see you're getting ready to get your hustle on dog," Whoopee Do said to Bill.

"I see you're getting ready to get your hustle on too," Bill responded with a smile. "What's going on? What's been cooking Whoopee Do?"

"Oh, ain't nothing cooking but the peas in the pot and they won't be cooking 'til the water gets hot," Whoopee Do poetically replied. "You know they gon start letting me get SSI, man?!! This is gon help me get my life back together , Dog, and get me back off the streets real soon, man!" He then flipped his semi-serious tone and asked Bill, "Hey, what did the dog say when the train ran over its tail?" Bill said he didn't know and Whoopee Do replied, "It won't be long now!" Just like a split in personality, Whoopee Do came back to being semi serious again. "It seems like every time I come down this way, you out here blowin yo horn!"

"If I'm not out here, there won't be anyone out here for me, so yep...I'm always out here blowing my horn, making a name for myself, Dollar Bill!"

"I know that's right!" Whoopee Do responded with an expression of certainty. "For Whom The Bell Tolls,"[11] Bill thought, as he envisioned the character in the story that was there to toll the bell at a certain time everyday no matter what.

---

[11] A book by Ernest Hemingway

WHOOPEE DO

Whoopee Do was an OG living and hanging
In the streets, always in the Hood Up to no Good
Playing it cool and acting tough..
Spent most of his time on cloud nine
With the instant flight of a drink or a puff
Panhandling to get high or something on the cuff
He would stand around on a corner of the busy downtown
Begging passersby who would walk down the streets
To spare him some change to get food to eat
Many of them gave donations to the destitute life
He claims to have led, but if they said "No"
He would stalk them and continue to beg..
His face was contorted into a pout
Mad at the world because his problems never pan out
His eyes were dilated and swollen like a bug
As if he'd been up all-night or high on drugs
He walked with a quick dip in his hip
He felt he was on point at being female slick
His conversation was quick
And very seldom went beyond getting with a chick
But, what kind of girl would want to walk that path
He always smelled like he needed a bath
His teeth were heavily stained with yellow markings
From the brown nicotine of the white cigarette smoke
His hair was nappy and his face was bumpy
And as he opened his mouth to speak
You would step back fifty feet
Because his breathe was hot and funky

71

He was a heavy smoker but never bought himself
a pack of cigarettes...
He smoked OPB's (Other People's Brands)
And would offer up a quarter for one of yours
As his cigarette supportive outlet
He came from way back in the hood
And even back then he was up to no good
Wherever he goes trouble follows
Many bitter pills he's had to swallow
He superstitiously believed that some old enemy
Or friend had stuck him with a voodoo pin
He always seemed to portray a dark-side persona
With a sneering grin
Never letting anyone get close or on his good side
Mainly because of his own false pride
But he socialized freely ith friends who were dope fiends
Their life revolved around drug abusing schemes
They were clever conniving thieves
Who could skillfully steal knots out of knees
And bites out of fleas
A lottery ticket gives no assurance
Of good or bad luck
But it is a guarantee that
These dope fiend thieves
Could be trusted just about as far
As you could throw a truck..
And as Whoopee Do stood in the
Dim light reflection
He portrayed the persona of a little professor
Scheming to get something for nothing
With slight hand of ease
He was dedicated to keeping
The beat of the streets

Doing well at times and on his feet
And other times he would fall behind
As life became tough
Like a steep mountain climb
Or your first walk on a tightrope line
Keeping an unsteady balance
Always in a paranoia state of mind
Looking back for the shrewd and wicked hand
Of fate followed by a stumble and fall
From the mountain climb
And the walk on the tightrope line
And a swift kick in the behind
By the familiar reality of hard times
His life was not like the sweet taste of wine
That gets better over a period of a time
Instead it was much worse
Finally relief would arrive
Like water quenching his thirst
Sometimes he would make a big score
But most of the time the hustle and bustle
Would produce only nickels and dimes
But from the Hood where he grew
This was the only life he knew
And from the starting gate
The race was already seeded
With Destruction and hate

Drug abuse and addiction lays out a very alluring, bright, red carper that leads to an unconditional destination of failure and downfall. The up and down side of life is a typical routine for many who seemed trapped in a vicious cycle of resistance to change with their backs against an unrelenting brick wall. It is a fact of reality. They are the have-nots. And for many of them, living a life in and out of jail, and daily drug and alcohol abuse is their way of doing something about it, their way of getting out.

Whoopee Do was wearing a shabby, out of season, brown coverall with tall, black, dingy boots, and a tightly tied black do rag around his head.[12] He illegally held a forty-ounce can of beer in his left hand.[13]   His advantage was that the Deputies of the Riverfront were not very strict. However, if you posed a problem while drinking illegally on the streets, like being in a scuffle or starting a disturbance, a jail cell could be in your near future. Regardless, Bill knew his fate. He knew that Whoopee Do was lingering, waiting to panhandle and asking him or her for money during the course of the night. Bill normally gave a few of his donations to street people. He felt, well, it was donated to him. But, he did have a commodity to exchange. It was Musical Entertainment, a quid pro quo.

Bill rationalized Whoopee Do's situation and the state of homelessness as a whole by saying that people do what they know how to do. Even though some of the street people knew how to do more than what they did, they seem to now be fine with living on a dime. They've been ensnared in sort of a spider web situation, which many people don't understand. Some sympathize with them, but do nothing. Some offer up their pity with a small contribution. Moreover, some share a genuine, human compassion for them. Either way, they were considered a burden to our well to do society and a disgrace when visited on by a world that did not know their struggle. With that in mind, Bill felt a sudden compassion as Whoopee Do slowly walked down the street

---

[12] The **do rag**, Which became popular among the Black Males, was introduced by rock n' roll legends Chuck Berry and Little Richard during the height of their fame. They wore the do rag to protect their carefully processed hair. Many Black people then and now even want their hair to be straight like White people's hair. Perming or processing naturally curly hair to make it straight was the way to go.
[13] Drinking alcohol outside of public premises, on the street, was against city ordinance at that time.

begging for handouts. There are many, he thought, like him, and some far worse. But, they were human beings, man and woman, given the same physical detail and attributes that we all have and depicts who we are.

Humanity however is merely a concept in which we inherit from birth, whereby we strive to achieve and maintain within the structure of our life, as we live by the criteria of society's given guidelines of morality. But, some of us have become desensitized and dehumanized through means of greed, lust, wrong choices, and perhaps, circumstantial experiences. Bill had learned through his own life experiences of trouble times that when he turned to GOD for forgiveness he was never turned away. GOD will forgive us for our sins if we completely bare our soul to HIM and repent, so the Bible says.

Although he was not a religious practitioner, Bill did read the Bible. He grew up like most Americans. He often reflected on the things he learned over the years in his readings. One lesson Bill always seemed to recall was the lesson of forgiveness, how it is better to give than to receive.[14] He did his best to practice this. Working as a band director with children in a local St. Louis School District, he would always forgive the students for their disobedient behavior. But, as people transcend from childhood into adulthood, some of our inappropriate behavior follows us and we still need forgiveness. We sometimes find it difficult to forgive one another for unacceptable behavior, or trespasses against us. Yet, we wish to be forgiven for our own actions of inappropriate behavior.

Bill settled into his playing spot. He began a whisper of sound into his saxophone and began the ballad of *Song Bird* by Kenny G, setting the mood for late night music lovers. With the magic touch of gentleness and the powerful emotion of sound he was bound to make you feel what he felt. "If only the world could feel the same," he thought.

The beat on the street picked up as the bars and clubs began to close. People still wanted to dance! They were not interested in the fun of the night coming to an end. They continued the part in the streets as Bill

---

[14] Acts 20:35

entertained them with his musical golden pipe. But, the deputies were soon instructing people to leave. After all, it was three o'clock in the morning.

He walked the short distance to his home and was soon in his apartment. He carefully removed his saxophone from the duffle bag and emptied the contents of donations onto his bed to count. He had many, many one-dollar bills, an abundance of fives, along with a few twenties and a mountainous pile of loose change. As he began to count the paper money, he came to a wad of bills that were balled up. When he pulled them apart he was shocked! His eyes could hardly believe what they saw! There in his hands were a bunch of five hundred dollar bills! "Why?? Who? Who could have been so generous? Who would have been so generous??" Bill couldn't come up with an acceptable explanation for this good fortune that had befallen upon him. He had to conclude that he'd never know. Blessings often come in disguise. Bill was elated, and then worry crept in. "Are these real bills or could they be counterfeit?" He quickly regained satisfaction and gratitude because just as he wouldn't know who gave this large amount of money to him, if it turns out to be fake, it's all fate. All Bill could think about now was all the bills he could pay off that were long overdue. He could get his rent caught up to date and he could possibly get his car fixed finally that had been broken down for several months. When Bill first came back to the Lou from New York his car broke down, so he took it to be repaired. The mechanic gave the automobile a quick and brief examination. He then noticed the New York license plates on the car and asked Bill with a puzzled look on his face, "Did you drive this car here from New York??" When Bill answered, "Yes", the mechanic replied, Then, *Jesus Christ* HAD to have been sitting in the passenger's seat!" Bill reflected. This may have very well been true for he surely felt blessed today! He looked up at the white ceiling towards the fast spinning ceiling fan and shouted out loud, "**THANK YOU LORD**!!"

Chapter 10

THIS IS WHAT I DO

The cumulus clouds were depicted as a perfect picture of heaven while Marlys looked through the porthole of the 747 entering the landing port at the St. Louis Lambert Airport. She was returning home from a four week concert tour. She had been to Europe, the countries of England, Russia and France. This was her first experience of leaving her own country. She saw the famous Eiffel Tower of London, the Kremlin in Moscow and the wonder city of Paris. She dined in the fabulous cafes and drank the finest of champagne and chardonnay. She took extensive walks through the city and shopped at the expensive clothing stores purchasing gifts for her loved ones back home. She spent endlessly on items for her children, sister, her mother and her closest friends.

After she set herself up, Marlys moved her mother into a beautiful home in the suburb of Creve Coeur so they could have closer contact. Her children spent many days and nights at their grandmother's home when their mother was traveling and caught up in the rapture of show business.

When Marlys was away from home she missed her family and friends tremendously. She recalled the lyrics to a child hood song, *"Make new friends, but keep the old, one is silver and the other's gold."* Her new life brought about new friends and many other things in her life she never imagined having. However, nothing could take the place of her family. She enjoyed the pink Mercedes she drove, the beautiful home she lived in and the fabulous clothes of her wardrobe. She seemed to literally have it all...but, still she was not full-filled.

She often thought of her children's father. They had parted more than five years ago. Their relationship began to fall apart when she began to persistently pursue her music career. At the time, he could not come to terms with her nights of out and about the city, engaging with her entourage of friends and fans. She began to receive a lot of attention from other men as she gained more recognition in the field of music entertainment. Some wanted to be friends while others wanted to be more. The arguments grew between the two lovers and her mate always blamed it on her career. Of course, Marlys did not agree and refused to give up her dream of becoming a star, even if it meant she would no longer be with him. They began to see less and less of each other until he eventually disappeared from her life. Since that time she had not had a steady relationship, someone whom she could depend on. Being so busy with her career and with the children to take care of, she's hardly had time to meet anyone, let alone get intimately involved with them. Of course, there had been a few boyfriends here and there, but being the dedicated entertainer and mother that she was, her children and her career always took priority. But more and more, lately, she missed having an intimate relationship in her life. She hoped and believed that in time someone would come along.

She reflected on the musician she had met on the Riverfront. She thought he was very attractive, and was extremely interested in the living he made as a street musician. However, she didn't know if he was interested in her. She assumed that he didn't recognize her as the *Queen of Venus*, which was a good thing. She wanted to meet a man who would accept her for her and not because of her image and fame. Very often she became apprehensive about this when she met men who were attractive and posed a potential for intimacy. She tried to stop thinking of him like that. She did plan to contact him for her private party and engage his services of entertainment.

She pondered on her contract with Capitol Records. It was extended over a period of five years and was secured with legal provisions, which allowed her the privilege of being paid for her performances in advance before she began her show. She had acquired so much leeway in the industry and she was proud.

The 747 landed smoothly and soon she was walking into the airport terminal where she saw her mother, sister and children awaiting her arrival. The terminal was also filled with men and woman with cameras, microphones and intrusive faces. The added attraction of Paparazzi waiting to take pictures and ask ongoing questions for their articles of news reports and magazines was not an exciting addition to her life. Although she had become accustomed to the attraction and attention she received as *The Queen of Venus* and enjoyed the flashing of cameras and the list of questions, but she wanted peace and quiet time with her loved ones. She wanted to hurry and get away. Her four-week tour of Europe had left her exhausted and she dreamed of the comfort of home.

There it was…the brightly colored displays of the paparazzi. Flashing cameras and pushy reporters began to bombard her. "How could she turn them away?" she thought. Marlys politely gave in to the inspiration of the moment. She put her hands on her hips and began to vogue. The photographers loved her dramatic flair as they moved closer to get a better shot. She gave them a show. Once the excitement settled she hurried along with her family and into a waiting limousine headed home in.

Chapter 11

THE TEACHER

On the other side of town Bill reminisced on his life as he prepared for his next student, Tommy. He and Tommy went quickly from stranger to friend meeting during the times Bill played around the downtown area. Bill learned a great deal of things in his travels, experiences and from his studies. He knew how important practice was so he practiced a lot. He thought about a few of his instructors who help pave the way for him. There was the firm style of Ms. Judy Pynn and the unlimited approach of Mr. Randy Thomasello; the talented Dr. Alvin Curtis and the late great Jimmy Cheatham. As a student and a young musician he relied heavily on his musical instinct as well as the guidance of his teachers. They taught him how to use his instinct and he eventually came to a place of confidence. He worked hard, and fortunately for him, the great examples that came through his life along the way where a part of his destiny. Bill knew himself to be very able and very capable of playing all around, and had, with some of music's greatest artists. He kept wonderful memories of some of his very first mentors and now he himself was a mentor.

Music was a true passion and blessing for him. The roads that led him to playing on the streets of St. Louis were vast and Bill couldn't image changing anything that happened to him in his past. There were some damn good times and some *got*-damn worse of times, some of the time. However, *everything **happens for a reason.** He* lived by that motto, and with everything that had happened to him, he had come to love his life. Sure, some of life's circumstances didn't have to happen and sure, there could have been better or easier times, and there was of course, but Bill learned long ago that what doesn't kill him makes him stronger. That's how he felt about his life and about things in general. Strong! Sure! Determined! He consciously reflected that feeling in his music and loved to share the knowledge that he accumulated over the years with others. And Bill didn't care how old the "others" were. He would find himself dropping musical knowledge on a little kid one day, and the next day dropping knowledge on someone old enough to be his granny!

Later that afternoon Tommy arrived for his lesson. Bill listened while he played a scale exercise on his saxophone in the key of C major. He had been giving him lessons for several weeks now. Tommy brought several good points with him; he already knew how to play, he had a basic understanding of reading music notation. He was responsible enough to acquire his own method books and he seemed to practice while he was away from Bill. He always produced a good tone quality on the instrument. Bill appreciated his enthusiasm about becoming better on the saxophone. Bill spent more than an hour with him each time he came by for lessons. Also, through conversation and exchange of ideas, he came to realize that Tommy was very knowledgeable about the history of American Music.

Bill continued to coach him on how to hold his hands when manipulating the saxophone keys. "The object is to keep your hands in close contact with the instrument at all times when playing," Bill instructed. Tommy listened and took direction with a rare passion to learn, for someone of his age. And they say *'you can't teach an old dog new tricks.'* Tommy wasn't really all that old, but he was no spring chicken.

Tommy was enjoying the lessons he received from Bill. He was happy to be finally taking on his once buried desire to play the saxophone. As Bill did his thing, Tommy reflected on a parable he once heard from his grandfather who played the harmonica; 'Those that can't, **teach** and those that can, **do**. He was fortunate to have someone like Bill who was good at doing both, teaching *and* playing.

The lesson came to an end. There was another student waiting to take a lesson. Tommy gathered his books and put his instrument into his case. "I'll see you at the baseball game tonight, right?" he asked Bill as he headed out of the door. "Sure thing," Bill replied, "You be cool, now!"

As Tommy walked to his car parked in the front of Bill's apartment building, a beggar approached him and asked if he had any change to spare. He reached into his pants pocket and handed the young man several coins. The beggar thanked him and headed down the street.

Tommy had compassion for those who were less fortunate than he was, just like his teacher and musical mentor, Bill. Everyone had problems! Mankind share common problems, and the problems we share are greater than the problems that divide us; and the problems that divide us are really problems that we create.

Bill had a few hours to kill before his shift started at the Stadium. He headed down to BB's Jazz Blues and Soup Club to grab a bite to eat, listen to some good music and to enjoy the pleasant atmosphere with comrades.

Chapter 12

FAMILY AND FRIENDS

Marlys kept an eye on the children as they spliced and splashed in and out of the swimming pool throwing hands full of water at each other. She partitioned the pool off to keep the little kids from going into the deeper end of the water. As they played vigorously, Marlys was feeling at ease. She was enjoying the day with her family and friends whom she had invited over for a wonderful afternoon of fun and relaxation. She seemed to be doing three things at once; talking on the phone, watching the children and listening to her mother telling stories to the guests. Her mother seemed to always have so much to say, and her delivery was priceless.

"When I was a young," her mother began, "My mother and father would go out to see *Ike and Tina* Turner, *Chuck Berry* and *Oliver Sain* in East St. Louis. This was before they became famous. And did you know after he became famous Chuck Berry opened a record store on Easton Avenue? Well, it's now called Martin Luther King Drive. I bought records from that shop every chance I got! And back in the 60's the gray and black cabs that drove up and down Easton Avenue were free so I gots around!" she chuckled. "Also, there were streetcars that operated from electric cables strung high in the air on tall poles..." She shakes her head and smiles. "But, those good days are long gone now. Now, we got people, like my daughter and *Nelly,* singing and rapping this old crazy music and driving around in jeeps and pink Mercedes with black tinted windows. It's a wonder they can even see where they're going in them thangs!" Everyone burst into laughter and then someone exclaimed, "Ms. Adams you are so funny! You should have been a comedian or something! Now, we see where Marlys got her talents from."

Marlys called the children in from the pool, including the adults that were also swimming. Her maid brought out trays of food and began serving sandwiches, cakes, cookies, chips and cold drinks of ice tea and soda. She told the children that after they finished their meals, she had candy for them. One of the adults yelled out with a smile, "What about me?"

Being with her kin and comrades were those pivotal and unsurpassable moments that meant everything to Marlys. She cherished the quality time she spent with the ones who knew and loved her the most. She surely had enough of whatever she needed, and it felt good to be in a position to give, because she didn't always have it like that. Her conviction that she could fulfill her dreams, just as anyone could, had at last come true and fate had been kind to her. All of the perseverance and hard work had paid off. She had become what she wanted to be and *so could anyone else.*

Chapter 13

FROM PRINCESS TO QUEEN

The Cardinals had won five consecutive games and were headed to Detroit to play against the Tigers. It was time to put the stadium at the bottom of his list of gigs. Bill moved around the city, playing at other venues and store fronts.

It was a Tuesday evening as Bill ended his night of playing in front of the President Casino on the Riverfront. He began walking towards the Metro Link Terminal on The Landing. Two women came from under the bridge. "Hey Music Man," they yelled. "We've got something for you." They began running to catch up with him. Bill recognized them. They were homeless and hung out in the area. They pulled some clothing items from a bag. They held two shirts in their hands that were decorated with music symbols. One shirt had a saxophone printed on its front. They wanted $10.00 for the two shirts. Bill handed them $10.00 and purchased the shirts. One of the women had a distinct southern accent and Bill asked her where she was from. "I'm from New Orleans," she said, "and they play music in the streets just like you be doing. Play a song for us, man," she continued. "Can you play *When The Saints Go Marching In?* I hear you playing downtown when I walk by all the time!" She smiled, showing her un-kept oral hygiene and Bill smiled back at her and said, "I can't right now. I've got to catch the train somewhere, but you can catch me tomorrow in the neighborhood downtown and I'll play it for you." "That's what's up Music Man," she replied. The two women thanked him for the $10.00 and went back in the opposite direction of Bill, back to the unimaginable life under the bridge.

He saw the St. Louis Post Dispatch in a newspaper stand inside the train terminal and he purchased a copy. The front-page headline read: 'The Queen Of Venus, St. Louis's Hip-Hop Star, Returning Home From A Four Week Tour Of Europe'. Her CD *Fire In The Hole* was number one all over the country and there had been talk of her and rap star Nelly collaborating a concert at the Scottrade Center.

Bill read the article on the front page of the paper and thought to himself after gazing at a picture of the recording artist, "Man, what a beautiful woman… To have a girl like her would be *surely a dream come true…*" As he looked more closely at the picture his heart began to race. The pretty woman he was looking at in the paper was the lady he had met on the Riverfront; the Princess, as he so affectionately referred to her, in his own mind… **SHE** was *The Queen of Venus!* Bill's thoughts began to overwhelm him. He remembered that when they became acquainted with each other, he didn't know who she was. He felt so embarrassed. He wondered what she may have thought about him not recognizing her. He wondered if he would ever see her again and what he would say. He couldn't stop wondering; he almost missed his train, daydreaming. He tucked the paper under his arm to ponder and read later, and hurried to catch the train. Not many passengers where on the train so Bill was able to find a seat without effort. He opened the paper and stared at the picture once again. Still dumbfounded, he continued to dwell on the fact that the woman with the mellow and dreamy eyes and the sweetest of voices, the beautiful Princess from the Riverfront, was **The Queen of Venus.** A feeling of radiance enveloped him and he became inspired to compose:

MELLOW DREAMER

She's a mellow dreamer rolling along

She's got the kind of love

You'll hear in a song

She dreams of building castles

On her highway to happiness

Going to fill them up

With love, understanding and tenderness

And she wears a disguise

But when she opens her eyes

Then, you'll realize

She's a Mellow Dreamer

Dreamer, Dreamer, Dreamer

She dreams of joy and peace

In the world when wars come to an end

She dreams of honesty

She'll find in a new friend

She prays to God for giving her

Each new sunny day

But, until it comes along

She'll keep holding strong

And she'll keep rolling on

She's a Mellow Dreamer

Dreamer, Dreamer

Dreamer

If you believe in love

Your dreams can

Come true

You keep on

Holding on

And believe in

What you do

So, turn the problems

In your mind

Into beautiful scenes

Everybody in the world

Should have Mellow Dreams

And she'll always have

Beautiful dreams

As long as

Love is king

So mellow

She seems

With beautiful dreams

Let happiness ring

Chapter 14

I CAN'T GET STARTED

The parking lot on the corner of 14th Street and Clark Street was filled to capacity. The streets were relatively quiet as a few stragglers drifted in and out of The Scottrade Center. There were ticket scalpers on the corners selling hockey tickets to the patrons at a discount rate, yelling, "Tickets! Tickets! I've got your tickets here!" This day the St. Louis Blues were competing against Minnesota.

Bill sat on the 14th Street side of the Scottrade Center playing his horn. His horn rang out beautifully across the St. Louis air, and all in all he was expecting and hoping to make a pretty penny that day. All of a sudden, a scrubby looking man shaking a plastic cup stood a very short distance from him. Bill politely asked him to move down the street because he was interfering with his business. "Look Bill… 'The Music Man'… you don't tell me where I can work! I'll do something to you!" Bill looked at him like he was crazy. He had to be drunk or high, Bill thought. After all, he *was* being nice about it. Bill knew, being among street people, that in some instances you have speak to them in a language they understood. "Look here! You ain't gon' kill nothing and you ain't gon' let nothing die… YOU aint gon' do shit! Bottom line here is, you're begging and I'm trying to work!!" "This is what I do my brother," the man mumbled. "Listen man…I'm not your brother cause my momma didn't have you, ok?" Bill said, "and I'm not knocking what you do man, just do it somewhere else!" Then, the beggar filled with rage said, "I'll come over there and break your jaw!" Bill quickly became alert and recognized the belligerency in the man's words. Ooh…now it was ON! He said to the beggar in a matter of fact expression, "That's a threat, you bum! You don't make threats against somebody from the Lou…you gone get your face rearranged over here talking shit man!" Bill was livid, but quickly slowed his mental roll. "I oughta knock you into the middle of next week… but I'm not going to touch you, with your cup shaking crack head ass! You'll be the one sitting in jail! " A staff member by the name of Clarence came out of the Scottrade Center and asked the beggar to leave. He left without saying another word. "Are you OK," Clarence said to Bill. "I try to look out for you when those guys come around. I see them sometimes standing right up on you, and that's not cool. They can be rude, but keep doing what you're doing Music Man." He smiled then turned around and went back into the building.

The crowd came out after the first period for a smoke break. Some made their way over to greet Bill, shaking his hand and offering him hugs. Along with being hockey fans, they were also *The Street Musician's* fans. Bill began to lay down a funky rhythm with his saxophone. A group of women formed a circle and began dancing around to the groove he was laying down. A tall, young man came and stood beside him digging the sounds as well. Bill was feeling good. He looked up suddenly and noticed a rather heavyset young man quickly approaching him. Bill was thinking he was going to contribute a donation. To his surprise, the man stood directly above Bill and yelled, "Take that horn and stick it up your ass!" He quickly turned and walked away. Bill stood up and angrily responded, "I think it'll fit up your ass better!" The man who had been standing beside Bill quickly interceded, "Aye, aye...don't let that get next to you. No good heckler! Keep doing what you're doing Music Man. You're doing a good thing." He reached into his pocket and pulled out a wad of money and dropped a twenty-dollar bill into Bill's bag. Bill sighed, gained his composure and thanked him for the money and advice.

It started to rain so Bill quickly gathered his stuff and ran towards shelter. He noticed a long canopy he could play under a few feet away. A white man was playing his guitar at the other end of it. Bill made it over and began to regroup. No sooner than Bill sat down a security officer and the supervisor of the Scottrade Center came out, like *Johnny on the spot,* and requested that either he move to the eight-inch perimeter of the sidewalk or they will call the police. Bill asked if they would consider that it was raining. They both replied with a flat-out "No!" Bill knew they were serious. He actually had been handcuffed, arrested and thrown in the bullpen of the police subdivision at the Scottrade Center for refusing to go across the street to play before. He was issued a summons and released, but he knew his legal rights were clearly violated. However, as he pursued a complaint against the arresting officer with intentions of follow up it was brought to his attention by legal counsel that the record of the incident had been destroyed, or was never made, which made his chances of filing a law suit pretty much null and void.

Bill recalled reading a book titled The **Games People Play** by Eric Burns. It was a simplified version of the Freudian theory of psychoanalytic transactions of personalities. In the game one of the players receives a bad pay off. Bill instantly recognized this situation to be a game of power play and quickly decided that he was not going to be the one to receive the bad pay off. This could be accomplished with a simple solution, don't be one of the players. *It Takes Two* to play a game. So, he politely complied with their request and moved his bag and portable chair into the rain as his audience of hockey fans looked on in confusion and disgust. One the fans yelled out, "That's bullshit, man! How come you have to play in the rain and that *other* man don't?!?" They began handing Bill donations before he even started to play and went back into the building. As he was sitting down to start playing again, his horn fell from the strap around his neck. He quickly recovered it and blow into it, checking to make sure it was ok from the fall. To his disappointment, it wasn't. He desperately attempted to locate the problem, checking the previously repaired spots. He hoped to solve any malfunctions before another crowd from the game poured out. It seemed that he had been examining his instrument for hours and when he thought it was repaired he realized it still was not. Nothing he did seemed to work! The hockey fans began to exit the Scottrade Center as he continued to frantically find the defect in his horn. The next time he looked up the crowd had become very dense. Mostly, there seemed to be transients and drifters standing around on the sidewalk near the vent, trying to stay warm, harassing and begging the remaining hockey fans for money. Some of the derelicts were con artists, begging the fans for money by fraudulently soliciting for homeless children. There were also people passing out leaflets to solicit customers to nightclubs and restaurants. And *ole whitey*, the guitarist, was still chilling, playing under the canopy. The two *Johnny on the spot*s were nowhere to be found. *Fairness should apply to all and not just some.*

Actually, St. Louis is technically in the South, marking the border between the North and South. The South is renowned for their acts of racism. Missouri fought in the Civil War in the 1800's as confederates, who were the soldiers of the South, whereby they lost to the Yankee soldiers of the North. Today, St. Louis is among the most racially divided cities in the country. There is a monument that stands like a desolate unmarked grave at the triangular intersection of North Broadway Boulevard, Seventh Street and Howard. The monument represents the Big Mound used during historic times for Native American ceremonies[15]. This Mound was also used to auction Black people into slavery[16]. It impeded European construction and was eventually completely demolished by 1870. Corbin Thompson and Bernard M. Lynch were two of the main slave dealers in St. Louis[17]. Thompson boosted about having a suitable and well-kept slave quarters. Lynch's slave pens housed men and women together on dirt floors. There was no concern for separation or privacy. It was located on Fifth Street and Myrtle. It lay hidden and was not dismantled until 1963 when discovered during construction of Busch Stadium on site. Since the time of the Civil War great effort has been taken by Black and White people to rid the country of racism. The Government eradicated this behavior from federal and local law. Therefore, racism is officially dead. But, the ghost still lives on just as we still clearly hear the voice of *Tupac* in light of new rap songs.

---

[15] Indian Scrap Book 111; *nationalgeographic.com*
[16] This information is not listed in the St. Louis Archives as a reference source, but has been passed down by oral tradition through the black generations since slavery.
[17] *Discovering African American St. Louis Second Edition*: By John A. Wright

Bill began to walk slowly down 14th Street. He was worried, wondering how he was going to get his instrument fixed. He didn't have enough money for an over-haul. He thought that maybe he could obtain credit or make a loan. Music was his livelihood. He'd have to figure something out. It started to rain again as he reached his apartment and went up the corridor of stairs. Once inside, he again examined his horn. He still could not get it to work. He decided to let it go and wait to see what tomorrow brings. He turned on the radio, and his favorite song by The Queen of Venus was playing, *Fire In The Hole*. He liked the rhythm and the sexually suggestive lyrics. Then, Bill contemplated on what's *really* going on in the world of rap music today. He felt that much of the hip-hop and rap music communicates violence and explicit sexual lyrics. Some of the hip-hop female artists are deviating from this trend of market, however, and going more pop. Also, Bill didn't care for the disrespect he often heard in rap music. The truth is that music expresses what a person has lived. But, there are musical expressions that offer nothing to contribute to the enhancement of positive behavior. He thought, "Do something for your people, in the name of *GOD*[18]!" He remembered a passage in the bible from the book of Acts. It roughly stated that when *GOD* calls for

you on Judgment Day it will in be the voice *HE* has given you, the distinct language by which you speak your voice, the particular dialect that you speak the language of your voice in and you won't be able to take your precious possessions with you. If you don't believe me, then ask King Tut. His elaborate treasures of jewels and precious items of gold stayed behind sealed in a tomb buried deep in the ground for thousands of years that were eventually discovered and

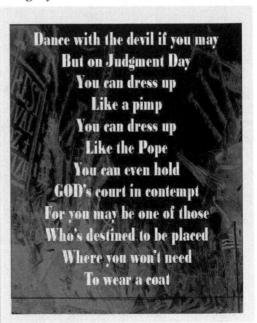

Dance with the devil if you may
But on Judgment Day
You can dress up
Like a pimp
You can dress up
Like the Pope
You can even hold
GOD's court in contempt
For you may be one of those
Who's destined to be placed
Where you won't need
To wear a coat

---

[18] Rap Star Snoop Dog has established and sponsored a children's football team for a number of years. This is an example of community contribution.

stolen by others and repossessed by the REPO Man.

Rap Star *Nelly,* accredited with putting St. Louis on the map, is quoted, along with other celebrities, during a TV discussion on the affects that hip-hop and rap music have on the young generation: "The record companies are only interested in making money..."[19]. This implies that the record companies have no interest in the affects of the music.[20] While this appears to be true, the interest that they may have on how the music affects the young generation seems to be secondary to the money that it brings in. However, as an artist *YOU* decide what message you want to get across in your music. ***Cash Rules Everything Around Me!***

The Black music artists of today flaunt the N-word around very negligently as it blares from cars and into the streets. Through power of communication it permits their listeners to defiantly continue to use the word with an okay message when relating to another Black person. But, when someone from another race calls a Black person the N-word they are offended and ready to result to violence. This is a clear example of false pride. Their rationality is that the N-word has a connotative meaning when used among Black people. However, there is no justification for using it in fun, casual play, or as profanity. Whatever the reason for using the N-word, the word carries baggage and causes harm. Also, it is not positively contributing to the community. It boils down to race exploitation when it is used to appeal to the negative side of people for profit, which is involved in including it in the recording of a great portion of rap music. With some Black people, the N-word (along with *motherfucker*) is heard in every other word of their speech. It may take a miracle to break this pattern. They just won't let the *nigger* die. Many Black adults have closed their eyes and ears to enlightenment. They are cool with how they speak and behave. It's a factor of their environment. They receive recognition from their peers and recognition is essential to our state of being as food is to our body, whether it is positive or negative.

---

[19] 2007 BET Awards

[20] Rap Star Nelly has made available full scholarships to students seeking to further their education. This is an example of community contribution.

Black people and rap artist who use the N-word appear to be progressing backwards and show no regards for the achievements of Martin Luther King, Malcolm X, Reverend Jesse Jackson, The Black Panther Party[21]. They all struggled to obtain political freedom as they presented themselves with freedom within. These political activists, as well as many others, dedicated their lives to bringing dignity and pride to Black Americans. While political freedom has relatively progressed, freedom is not just the right to do as others do; it also involves freedom of the mind. The chains that incarcerate many Black people's mind, for the most part, are still very present. Every time a Black person uses the N-word she or he is reinforcing the chains that hold their people back. So, before you criticize someone else's negative endeavors toward the Black race take a good look at *The Man In The Mirror*, for you may be one of those who are no better than the people who are criticized. It may take these particular Black people another two hundred years to improve their self-esteem. Change does not come over night, but if you choose to continue to use the N-word, then consider your intrusion onto the space of others who wish to project a positive image of themselves in a fast-pace and expanding society. Some Black people have resorted to referring to each other as dogs - *'What's up dog?'* This is another derogative step backwards. The word *dog* carries more baggage than the N-word. Black people that use the N-word and other words that project a negative image have been so scorned until it appears that they don't know how to have a positive image. Come on now! If you take a bath in the Muddy Mississippi River how could you expect your body to be clean? We should be doing as the leaders before us, considering the society we now live in, and lay the groundwork to eradicate this language from our children of the future so that they can learn to communicate with acceptable, universal diction and respect. Having a Black President of our country should mean more than something to brag about or criticize. All Americans need to take a *Pledge of Allegiance* in representation of his efforts to bring about *fairness for everyone and not just some*. This will give some of us positive self-esteem, which will help to generate a positive image in society.

Bill was appalled at the alarming number of Black people who walk the streets of downtown with no education, no job, begging for money,

---

[21] The Panther Party was started by Huey Newton and Bobby Seale for self defense On October 15, 1966. *www.blackpanther.org*

cigarettes, shaking cups, conniving and jiving passersby, standing at bus stops asking for transfers to resale, vaguely aware of other realities of the world, and never acquiring the social and economic skills of success to achieve the American Dream. Their children grow up lacking the sense of property value and do not experience the luxury of privileges. Children who come from wealth have privileges as they climb through the window of opportunity in America and are not allowed to fail. Other races that have come to this country in search of a better life have prospered and met success. However, the Black people are the only race in America who did not come to this country in search of a better life; they were torn from their mother country of Africa and brought here in bondage, striped of their culture, language and pride. The African women had to deal with fornication by means of rape in front of their children, whereby the term *motherfucker* was derived. Their children were born with various shades of color. The African men stood by as their manhood was so belittled until they started calling each other *man* in order to maintain some pride and to counter-act the degradation of being called *boy*. After hundreds of years the term *what's up man* still reverberate in the streets throughout our nation and so does the term *motherfucker*.

The Africans were denied the right to even an informal education. Many of them are still struggling with education and language. However, they have come to commonly speak in a very distinguishable dialect[22]. A clear example would be the differentiation in the pronunciation of the English language between Americans and British. The Government has appropriated programs that provide funding for education and vocational training for marketable job skills to those who are indigent. But, there are not enough people taking advantage of this opportunity. A large number of Black people do not believe in education. Their parents didn't have an education, nor did their grandparents. So, they go about life making it on their wits. Progress needs to be taken to inspire these particular people with the belief that an education is also for them and is the key to success. Black people are at the bottom of American Society and perhaps the world[23], and although this may be

---

[22] Also referred to as Ebonics, the spoken language from "The Hood" has developed into a very distinguishable idiom, referred to as Black Talk; also, a recording by jazz organist Charles Earland converted the Beatles' Eleanor Rigby into an anthem called *Black Talk*.

[23] *The Wretched of The Earth* by Franz Fannon

true in perception, WE know that there is gold in them there hills of the Hood. Dig deeper and you will also find it is true. Through the power of communication and music, artists could easily come together and do something collectively about this.

DON'T CALL ME A NEGRO

DON'T CALL ME A NEGRA

DON'T CALL ME AN AFRICAN

WITH AN AMERICAN AFRO

DON'T CALL ME COLORED

PEOPLE

FOR THIS TERM DOES NOT

DEPICT ME ...BUT, TO BE PUT

VERY SIMPLY WITHOUT

THE HAPPY FACE OF A TOE

TAPPING CARICATURE

I AM A BLACK MAN

LIVING IN THE LAND

OF AMERICA

Over the years of engaging with many fans while playing music on the streets, Bill often listened to their stories and problems of childhood, as well as their testimonies. Many suggest an unresolved conflict with their mothers. Many of them state that their mother was strung out on drugs and had lost custody of them, whereby they lived with their grandmother. But, in many cases you couldn't talk to grand momma either because she also was out on the corner patting and turning. They had developed a lack of respect for various reasons in their upbringing as a child. In most situations the father was not there or seldom seen; he may not have been a crucial part of the child's life. As adolescents they learned to idolize pimps, gangsters and drug dealers in the hood because they appeared to be the only ones who were making it. The lack of fathers in the households of today may be a primary contributing factor to a growing, major social problem among the youth population. He thought, the negative attitude that the youth of today seem to harbor and support, comes from their childhood and is subconsciously dragged into their young adult life, and is projected onto society therefore, generalizing women in regarding respect. It is clearly verbalized, dignified, amplified, characterized and recognized in the way rappers write their raps.

Bill climbed into his queen size bed. He could hear the pitter patter of raindrops tapping against the windowpane. He spent a lot of his time alone and pondered often in thought. Brain…Be still, he thought, as he soon drifted off into a dream of a place far away from North Broadway.

Chapter 15

BILLY JUNE

As a kid, Bill's family members and friends called him Billy June. He could remember being exposed to blues music in St. Louis at a very young age, memories of seeing the Great B. B. King, who played at local bar in his neighborhood. He sometimes would sneak in through the front door of the bar without being noticed. If he did get noticed, he quickly got the boot. When that happened he remembered going to the back door, which was usually always opened. He would listen to the real blues and it reminded him of church; listening as the people would moan and shout words of sorrow and prayers. He also could remember venturing into the red light district, called Gas Light Square. He saw a host of diverse musical entertainment and people there from so many interesting and intriguing cultural backgrounds. His young eyes didn't miss much.

Young Billy June was introduced to jazz and blues through his family members and through the overall environment in which he was raised. As a child, someone around him was always playing it. He also came to enjoy classical music and especially loved listening to it on the radio. He felt it had sharp contrast to the blues and jazz that he normally heard. His father listened to a lot of country music, but blues and rock n' roll were his favorites. This was the 60's. This was the time of the Hippy Movement in St. Louis. This was the beginning of young White adults openly engaging with Blacks, and music was the center of that new friendly association. As Billy June grew into a young man, he recognized that it was music that brought people together without prejudice. He was cultivated in the fact that music and people just coincide well. It bridges gaps. It was the nature of social and cultural mingling. With music as the host, the tensions of racial problems appeared non-existent. The moments became about a time of release and liberation for all. The white people in the 60's felt the excitement and the electrifying spirit jazz and blues gave them and they were charged. Subsequently, the music changed the world creating a significant cross-over.

Billy June had two sisters and a brother. His older sister Gwendolyn married and had three daughters. His younger sister Michele had a son. She died an untimely death at the age of 36. His brother Marlo married and had three sons. He also had a son and daughter out of wedlock. His parents, Laura and William, were not musicians themselves, but their family members were very musically inclined. His mother had brothers who performed as a local singing group and they also sang in church with the great gospel leader Bobby Jones. At that time and before his rise to fame, Jones was the choir director at their local church in Baden.

Billy June's father was the first cousin to the great legendary rock n' roll man Chuck Berry, whose contributions to our society made a vast mark in American History. Louis Armstrong is known as the very first innovator of American Music. He exposed America to jazz improvisation. Charlie Parker contributed to the American listeners, as well as abroad, a style of jazz called be-bop. John Coltrane contributed a style of music that was very dissonant and spiritually inclined. One of his albums said it best. It was a French term label called *The Advant Garde*, meaning *on the edge*. Just like these jazz greats, the remarkable Chuck Berry showed the people an easier way than jazz to play American music called Rock n' Roll.[24] The common factor among these musicians is that they innovated in the blues.

Bill's father had a daughter from a previous relationship. Her name was Karen. She was the daughter of Ms. Irene Clark, a well known educator in the city of St. Louis. They lived in very closely knitted German town called Baden. Bill knew her during his early childhood. Both of Bill's Grandmothers resided in Baden, Thelma Berry and Ellen Eddins. The city of Baden cradled the roots of rock n' roll's hall of famer, Chuck Berry! Baden is also the home of former Senator, William Clay Sr. the first Black Representative from Missouri[25], who served in the House for more than three decades.

Ellen was the daughter of William Robinson[26]. He was of the 4th

---

[24] Rock and Roll was quickly adopted by the European-Caucasians and they passed it off as their own music. Also see a 1987 film, Chuck Berry: *Hail! Hail! Rock N Roll*

[25] History.house.gov

[26] The Robinsons were sharecroppers, which was an elevated form of slavery where the workers stayed in debt to the land owner. Today, modern slavery has been extended to poverty.

generation. Sammy was of the 1st generation. His grandmother was from Africa. She was taken from Africa at the estimated age of fourteen and brought to England under slavery. From England, she was brought to the United States under slavery and lived in Big Bee Valley, Mississippi. She had a daughter who bore a son named Sammy. William Robinson married a woman named Annie Miller who was part Choctaw Indian. They had six children; Artence, Ellen, Annie, Ollie, Mack, and Odell. Ellen married a man named Nickolas Dancy. They bore a daughter named Laura. Laura's father Nickolas was killed in a train accident. Ellen had another daughter named Ann and then she later married a man named Levi Eddins who was a bootlegger and moved to Columbus, Mississippi. Ellen bore three sons while in Columbus. From there she and her family moved to Baden seeking a better life. Ellen continued growing her family having three more daughters, Mary Ann, Gail, and Sheila, and then later in life, another daughter named Melanie.

Ellen's oldest daughter Laura met her husband to be, William Richardson, the son of Thelma Berry, growing up in the city of Baden. They married and had four children; William (Billy June), Gwendolyn, Michele and Marlo. Laura was a Stay At Home wife and mother until her children were mature. After they grew up and left the home she began to work in the field of home service.

Thelma was the daughter of William Berry. William Berry was of the 1st generation. His mother was an African woman who escaped slavery in Memphis. She came to Missouri with an Indian man from Oklahoma[27] who was a gardener on a plantation in southern Missouri. William Berry married a woman named Lucinda and they had a son, Henry. When Lucinda died from an illness, he later married a woman from Iowa named Lavenia Hutchinson. Lavenia attended Fisk University. Her mother, who was from Kentucky, was named Laura. Laura was Irish and Indian but was listed as mulatto. Lavenia's father was from Virginia and his father was from Africa. Lavenia was mulatto. William and Lavenia had three children; Atwell, Clarence, and Thelma. Thelma's first son was named Stanford. She then had two more sons and a daughter; William, Hutchinson, and Dorothy. William was born William Berry,

---

[27] *The Autobiography,* by Chuck Berry

but after he grew up, he changed his name to his father's name, Richardson. William's father was Ocee Richardson and he was from Georgia. Ocee died when William was at a very young age, and the only father that he knew was his uncle, Henry Berry. William (Berry) Richardson served in the United States Army during the Korean War. His first marriage was to a young woman who died early from cancer and they bore no children. William then married Laura Dancy (Bill's Mother) at the age of twenty six and is remembered to have been a hard working, honest man and a good family provider.

Everyone surrounding Billy June in his Baden Community were either relatives or very close, like family, through generations of friendships. Their families were the original Black people of Baden. The children of Baden lived in a community where the white public schools in the neighborhood had never had any Blacks to ever attend them. In 1954 the Federal Government lifted the ban of education segregation mandating the Civil Rights of Black Americans to receive an equivalent education to White Americans. Before the mandate, the Blacks in Baden were bused to Black-Only schools further out in the city. Missouri resisted at first, but in 1955 it was forced to enact upon this law. In 1956, Billy June was among the first Blacks to attend the schools in his neighborhood. Their attendance at the Baden School was ground breaking for them and their families, but it brought about resistance with many White parents. They stood along the streets holding signs of protest and shouting: "Niggers Go Home. This is our school." The Black children and parents were continuously harassed and intimidated. They were called out of their names over and over again, day after day, but the secret weapon that the Black community had was faith and perseverance. They held hands tightly as they marched from their homes, parading down the middle of the menacing street of North Broadway projecting the slogan, "We Shall Overcome"[28] White children, mothers and fathers stood along the sidewalks screaming and yelling in protest. Their government officials and police officers didn't protect them but they determinedly continued to stride in the path of justice until these outlandish and intimidating conditions were eventually subdued. The Black people of Baden attended their community churches and were taught to forgive the people who protested their right to an equal education, for they know

---

[28] The song We Shall Overcome was written by folk musician Pete Seeger. He introduced the song to Martin Luther King during the Civil Rights Movement.

not what they do[29].

When he was a teenager, Billy June moved to Milwaukee, Wisconsin with his parents who were in search of a better life. He later attended the University of Wisconsin-Oshkosh. He majored in music and studied the saxophone with Doctor Alvin Curtis. He spent a lot of time in the practice rooms working on technique and studying chord progressions on piano. He gained a profound understanding of harmony during this time. He gained a name for himself in the scene and passed through many bands of different musical styles. People started calling him 'Dollar Bill', which depicted his musical character; a dollar bill goes from hand to hand as Bill went from band to band.

While doings gigs and hanging out in Madison, Wisconsin, he met a Professor and musician by the name of Jimmy Cheatham. He taught band classes and jazz improvisation technique at the University. Bill *knew* of him! He was a re-known trombone player from New York City in the 1950's. He had lived the history of American Music. Jimmy and his wife Jeanie used to work with one of the most famous Ragtime pianist - composers of the 20th century musicals, Eubie Blake, at one point in his career. He worked with The Jazz Messengers, who were one of the most influential groups in the creation of progressive jazz, and he did a duet with jazz trumpeter Red Rodney who is acclaimed to have been one of the best of the first bebop trumpeters in America! He worked a lot with the prolific jazz drummer and bandleader Chico Hamilton, and even the great saxophonist Ben Webster.

Jimmy approached Bill while Bill was playing in a club and told him he had a great sound. Bill let him know that he was related to Chuck Berry and in response he told Bill that music was *"in his blood"*. He invited Bill to come to the University and sit in his classes and share his sound of music with the students. Bill felt honored and obliged, eventually becoming a student himself. He assigned Bill many chromatically based patterns from saxophonist Oliver Nelson[30]'s book, *Jazz Patterns*. Bill would work quickly master the pattern, but Cheatham was not

---

[29] More than fifty years later the students in the County of Ferguson, Missouri are fighting for their right to obtain a equal education

[30] Oliver Nelson was also from St. Louis.

interested in hearing it. His simple response was, "I knew you would get it. That's why I gave it to you." He told Bill that patterns weren't meant for playing out; they were meant to help him get his hands together. "You have your own story to tell. So, when you wake up in the morning," he continued, "let your horn be your cup of coffee. It goes right along with washing your face and brushing teeth." He informed Bill that, the great saxophonist, Lester Young told him to "get an education". So, he did, and now Cheatham wanted to encourage Bill to continue doing the same thing...learning! Bill began to do engagements with Cheatham and his wife Jeanie, who was a great pianist. One day Bill asked Cheatham about setting up a rehearsal and Jimmy asked Bill what was keeping him from rehearsing. He didn't believe in group rehearsal too much. He claimed that it affected the spontaneity of the music. Cheatham believed in individual preparation. He told Bill of a story about jazz pianist Thelonious Monk. He hired a saxophone player for a gig and told him where to go and rehearse. The saxophone player went the place of rehearsal. He waited for two hours, but no one showed up. He called Thelonious Monk on the phone to find out what was going on. Thelonious Monk told him that the rehearsal was for him. Everyone else was already rehearsed. Jimmy also disclosed to Bill a story about the great sax player Ben Webster. Ben had developed a serious mental defect that filled him with a lot of rage and anger that made him difficult to be around, so rehearsals didn't work too well. However, the minute he picked up his horn and blew into it, the air and his energy was beautiful and sweet!

After several years of teaching at the University of Wisconsin-Madison, Jimmy Cheatham decided to go back to New York. He asked Bill to come back with him, so Bill packed up the minimal items that he had and headed for the 'Big Apple'. This was his second stage of music education.

When Bill was not gigging with Jimmy, he gigged with other musicians and explored New York. Playing with Cheatham gave him an opportunity to explore the country side. One important gig brought him back to his home town of St. Louis. They were scheduled to appear at the Space Night Club for a weekend engagement. Jimmy's wife Jeanie, who was the keyboard player for the band, became ill with pneumonia after their previous gig in Chicago. Another local female pianist was called to replace her. Her name was Carolyn and she came highly recommended. She came to the gig and did an excellent job playing, and getting Bill's attention. She and Bill quickly became the best of friends and lovers. When the gig ended, Bill went back to New York, and the two love birds promised to keep in touch. They talked extensively on the phone and Bill visited her every time he came back to St. Louis. One day he woke up very zealous with Carolyn on his mind. He called her up and the very first words that came from his mouth were *"we can make it if we try with Just the Two of Us"*. She was elated and of course agreed. He made plans to move back to St. Louis to be with her. The plus was that he would also be closer to his family. He and Carolyn formed a jazz band and played the local club circuit. Bill felt the St. Louis scene failed in comparison to playing the club scene in New York which is re-known for its fabulous cabarets. But they built up their reputation in the city and a large following of fans.

Carolyn was a very beautiful woman to Bill. She reminded him of the legendary jazz vocalist Billie Holiday who was known for wearing a white Magnolia in her hair. Carolyn wore a red rose in her hair, and when she performed she dressed very elegantly. There was one flaw in her personality as Bill came to realize; Promiscuity. She didn't honor their commitment to each other so their relationship began to fall apart. They argued often and she proved herself to be the supreme of drama queens. She would secretly talk on the phone and leave the house abruptly with no explanation. Eventually, Bill saw her with another guy. They were standing in the moonlight embraced in each other's arms, like dark romantic silhouettes in the picture reflection of a shaded window. He was sick about it, but he pretended to not have seen what he most defiantly saw.

LOVE IN THE BLIND

There was a man
Who thought he had a love so true
He did everything for his girl
That a man is supposed to do
Until one day he saw things
He didn't understand
She was in the arms of another man
He thought that if he told himself a lie
The things that he saw would pass on by
So he covered up his eyes
And he tried to pretend
He would have her love Until the end
He didn't heed the warning
When he saw the sign
Thought he could have Love in the blind

People talked, Didn't have to wonder
What they talking 'bout, but he wondered
What would he do if his friends found out?
But his friends, if they really knew
Did only what friends normally do
Talked about how he knew the rules
But he thought he could keep his girl
By playing a fool... So he covered up his eyes
And tried to pretend
He would have her love Until the end
He didn't heed the warning
When he saw the sign
Thought he could have... Love in the blind

Didn't you see the sign?
Didn't you see the sign?
It was telling you to
Leave that girl behind

Didn't you seen the sign?
Didn't you see the sign?
You thought you could have
Love in the Blind

Look in the mirror so you can see
Just what you're going through
The sun is shining, but
Rain keeps on falling on you
Now that girl's no longer by your side
Can't you see that
She was taking you for a ride?
With her, you held your head up high
But tell me...What you're going to do
Since she said good by
He covered up his eyes
And he tried to pretend
He would have her love Until the end
He didn't heed the warning
When he saw the sign
Thought he could have Love in the blind

Obviously Bill couldn't stay with Carolyn after this. Before he only suspected…now he knew without any doubt. He ended their relationship. She joined another band and Bill was left with bittersweet memories. She wronged him, but she was already in his system. Bill still wanted to try to work things out, and time after time he tried to win her back. Eventually, he finally concluded that he could no longer afford her anymore opportunities for redemption. Like a bridge over troubled waters, it was time for him to move on. He jumped ship and let the ship hit the Titanic Iceberg.

I FEEL NO PAIN

I feel so cold
You know my life just ain't the same
I used to be a warm hearted man
Now it feels like water is in my veins
I was a good man
Thought I had a good woman
But the way she treated me I didn't see it coming
The rain keeps falling putting water in my eyes
But I don't feel nothing I can't even cry

I feel no pain
Every since that woman
Left me standing in the rain
I feel no pain
It seems like the falling rain
Has washed my pain down the drain

She spent up all my money on her friends
Like it came down from heaven above
She went to all the high-class parties
Even showing her love at the club
She drove a BMW and had a closet
full of Gucci designs
But she took my love for granted
when she started giving other men her time
She started cheating on me
Creeping with Joe and Tyrone
I even caught her with my best friend
He taped them making love on his cell phone

I feel no pain
Every since that woman
Left me standing in the rain
I feel no pain
It seems like the falling rain
Has washed my pain down the drain

Every time a party began
You know she wanted to entertain my friends
It kept tearing us apart
But she kept on breaking my heart
Coming in late at night
Then she wanted to fuss and fight
When there were beautiful stars above
How could this be true, true love

I know I'm going to surrender
On one these cold lonely nights
But it's got to be to some loving arms
That's going to treat me right
She don't have to be a pretty thing
Cause true beauty the eyes don't see
But while I'm taking care of her
All she's got to do is take care of me

I feel no pain
Every since that woman
Left me standing in the rain
I feel no pain
It seems like the falling rain
Has washed my pain down the drain

Chapter 16

THERE'S NO LOVE LIKE A MOTHER'S LOVE

Bill found a new hot spot on North Broadway, the Royal Palace Hotel, to perform a solo act with pre-recorded music. The hotel was a popular location that drew in all types of people, ranging from airline stewardesses and big business affiliates, to other out of town entertainers and visitors from foreign countries. The city's working girls also found that this was a lucrative place to meet marks. This downtown section and hotel was known for catering to men with money.

When Bill wasn't playing for street crowds and teaching private lessons at home, he worked for a local school district where he taught music. Just recently, he moved to North County with his mother. This worked for two reasons; Bill could keep an eye on his aging mother, and at the same time, he could save up his money in order to get ahead of the game. Bill's mom Laura had always been a very responsible person. She never failed to look out for her children's needs and stood by all of them through difficult situations. Her home actually became sort of a halfway house because many people came and went. She was known to take them in and share their burdens until they could do better. Her son Bill was one of those people.

"Reach Out and Touch Somebody's Hand and Make This a Better World If You Can... " The virtue of compassion in this popular Diana Ross tune was the type of compassion Laura instilled in her children from day one... not through tenacious lessons or strict lectures, but from the nature of behavior she displayed.

A Mother's Love

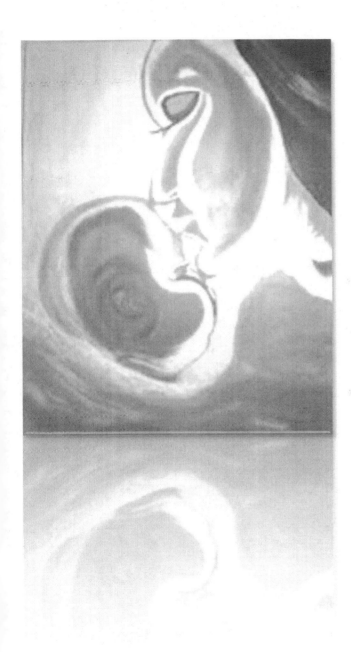

You can travel
The world
In a airplane
A rowboat
A horse
Driven
Stagecoach
In search
Of a good
Man
Or that
Special girl
The one that
You have been
Dreaming of

But believe
Me my friend
When search
Comes to an
End
And with
Wisdom of
Eyes
You will come
To realize
That there is
No Love
Like A
Mother's
Love

Bill played his saxophone at the Royal Plaza every Wednesday and Saturday night. Over time he gained a pretty nice following of fans. He would see the street girls come and go, working the scenes, seeking out customers while swaying and dancing to the *rhythm of the boogie, the beat*. Every now and then Bill would join them for a drink after a show. He found them genuinely easy to talk to and very down to earth. They always asked him to play the song *Ta Ra Ra Boom De-Ay*[31] so they could get up and dance...they even made up their **own** words to go with the melody. They became friends with Bill and would stay after the gigs sometimes to help him pack up his equipment. He would give them rides to their destinations, but never was it to their homes. Nice or not, they were working girls, so the next stop is either to meet a date or to score some drugs. They smoked crack and used heroin. Bill was pretty contented with having a drink here and there, and when they would invite him to join in on their drug use, he would refuse. Yet he didn't knock them for what they did. Prostitution is the oldest profession known to man. He reflected on the history of American Music, whereby when jazz began to develop in the brothels of New Orleans, its first audience of fans were prostitutes. Jazz bares no boundaries in its articulation of expression or in its extensive reach throughout the society we live, nor does prostitution. Sex is one of the most essential factors of human nature. The freedom of jazz reflects the intriguing, uninhibited lives of prostitutes, really, Bill thought.

Bill hired a vocalist by the name of Elise. He called her Billie Holiday. They vibed so well together that there was never a need for them to rehearse, and they never did. Spontaneity in music is one of the greatest accomplishments a musician can achieve. It bares the truth.

Bill and Elise made a great duet. They took on another weekly gig in Chesterfield at club Night Owl in addition to the gigs at the Royal Plaza. Bill felt, gigging with Elise was like riding in a drop top Lexus with his feet planted beneath the wheel, the wind blowing through her curly

---

[31] Ta Ra Ra Boom De-Ay is a Vaudeville song made famous by Lottie Collins and performed in London, England. The song's authorship was disputed for some years. It's ownership was accredited to Henry J Sayer, however he later admitted that he first heard the song in the 1880's sung by a Black singer called Mama Lou in a well-known St. Louis Brothel run by baby Connors. The song was used in a Television show called Howdy Doody.

locks of hair with her long, red manicured nails slightly gripping the dash as he accelerated through a green light...*Go For It!* Bill was single and he was attracted to her. However, there was, what Bill referred to as, an oil leak. She had a serious drinking problem, just like Billie Holiday had a serious drug problem. She was an alcoholic and made sure she got her fill at the gigs and at home. This eventually brought an end to the music. She committed herself to a treatment facility, which was a good thing, but Bill was left hanging. They had a following together. People came just because of her sometimes and without that chemistry between the two of them on stage together, Bill lost some of his gigs.

This was the beginning of a downward spiral. Bill felt discouraged, being out of work, and fell into a slight depression, refusing to follow up on any further ventures. He spent many nights at home digging through boredom. He soon became restless and he sought out his street girl friends. He began to make himself available to them to drive them around to their dates and to score drugs.

Three girls that Bill hung around with were Stacy, Kara and Rachael. Rachael was a tall with curly blond hair, with very attractive, model-like features. She dressed very classy and obviously made a good living at what she did. Kara was a very cute blond as well, but as tough as nails. She solicited, but she also created an opportunity for herself whenever she felt the need to do so. She had been known to mix in date rape drugs in her "client's" drinks. No sex needed with that plan. Kara would clean them out, taking their credit cards, jewelry, cash or anything with value, even their automobiles; taking them for joy rides around the city for hours before abandoning it. Stacy was a cute brunette. Bill didn't know very much about her. He had only seen her a few times. He concluded that she may be just along for the ride, maybe being schooled by the other two women.

Bill and the girls were driving around, hanging out. Stacy and Kara were in the back seat and Rachael was sitting in the front passenger's seat. Rachael made a quick call on her cell phone and instructed Bill to go to 14th Street and Cass Avenue. Bill pulled in front of a junk car lot and parked. A blue SUV pulled behind him and Rachael got out of the car and into the front seat of the SUV. After about 3 minutes, she got out of the SUV and climbed back into Bill's car. They pulled off heading south on 14th Street. "Ok, now take us to Benton and Gravois, Bill", Rachael said. They arrived in front of a two story brick home and they all went in. Rachael turned to Bill and said," Relax while I gather a few things, ok?" The other two girls disappeared into interior of the house. Bill looked around the room he was left alone in. It was elegantly plush and filled with beautiful furniture. Rachael had once told him that when she divorced she won a big court settlement. His guess was that the house must have been a part of the settlement.

As bill chilled, captivated by the attractiveness of his surroundings, Stacey and Kara came out dressed in lingerie. Bill blushed at how gorgeous they appeared. Their beautiful bodies were no illusion. Bill tore his eyes away long enough to then notice Rachael enter the room dressed in lingerie, flaunting her sexuality. She was carrying a silver tray with cups of water, a silver lighter, some syringes and a glass pipe. She immediately sat down beside Bill and placed the silver tray on a glass table that sat in front of them. She emptied several capsules into a spoon and added water to it. She took the silver lighter, flicked it and held it under the spoon until it began to sizzle from the heat. Then she dropped a small piece of cotton into the spoon, and picked up the syringes. She stuck the needle into the cotton and drew the liquid into the syringe. She then tied a black scarf around her left thigh and stuck the needle into her vain. She pressed down on the plunger of the syringe allowing the drugs to flow inside of her until it was all gone. She untied the scarf from around her thigh and let the red liquid draw back into the syringe several times, each time pressing it back into her vain. She dropped her head back and the balls of her eyes slowly rolled back until her lids closed, as if she was in heaven. She then opened her eyes, looked Bill in the face and smiled. He could see that her pupils were heavily dilated. She reached into her bosom and pulled out a wad of money and handed $500.00 to Bill. "These are my girls", she said with a sexy, but slow and slurred tone. "They work for me and I take care of them. You take care of us and the three of us will take care of you." No sooner than she finished that statement of clear fact, she went into a deep nod with her narrow chin touching the top of her voluptuous bosom.

Kara went over to the table and repeated the same routine... the capsules, water and the syringe. Stacy went to Bill and began kissing him on his lips. "I don't do smack," she said, "I only please men... and smoke a lil crack from time to time." At the mention of the word "*men*" Rachael came out of her nod. "I want you to spend some time here with us tonight Bill and if you need more money, I've got that for you too." She picked up one of the glass pipes, dropped a rock of crack in it and put it up to Bill's lips. "Take a hit," she said. She lit the lighter and melted the crack into the brillo tightly wedged into the tip of the pipe. Bill took a long drag on the glass. He held the smoke in his mouth for a length of time before exhaling. He then began to float with a tingling, euphoric feeling of sensation, as if he were in heaven. Each of the girls took a hit from the pipe. After they finished they began to caress Bill, rubbing his body with their delicate hands. Rachael began to kiss him and unbutton his shirt. He was captivated by her soft, feminine touch. It felt so right...but it wasn't just one pair of soft gentle hands...it was three. He became overwhelmed. It was a moment of pure bliss for him. But from that pleasurable moment of *Sexual Healing*, combined with the sensation and addictiveness of the crack, Bill's life gradually went from sugar to shit.

For six months Bill ran around with Rachael, Stacy, Kara and many of their friends. They exchanged money with him, paying him for his services; he spent most of his time with them, taking and picking them up from dates, taking them to score drugs and just riding them around the city trifling. Bill had become a reliable source for them. There were many days when his car was filled with street girls. He had totally neglected his music and was spending very little time at his mother's home. He had found a *New Love...* Crack...it had taken his life all the way out of sync. He began to meet up and hang around with a different class of people whose concern for the law was to violate it and not get caught. They were shrewd and unruly. They broke the law with the ease of a gracefully spinning ballerina dancer. The streets governed their lives. Hustling the streets was their daily routine, like a job, and for many of them, it was the only job they had, so work never ended, *Eight Days a Week*. And Bill's crack use quickly became a crack habit. It became a daily activity for him. Hanging out with the street girls, stepping into their world and leaving his world behind, was the new chapter in his life. What did it mean?

In the field of medicine, cocaine is classified as the most addictive drug.

But, this term "addictive" is merely a wicked ploy of incorporation manufactured by the crafty hands of design. In analogy, just as many under privileged children learn to play basketball in the street alleys of their neighborhoods, and just as the children of Minnesota learn to play hockey on the ice glazed streets of their neighborhoods, the children of South America and South Africa learn to be natural chemists. They are taught at a very young age how to blend vegetation from the soil in order to control a person's behavior. Within a few months, they are able to make their own crack out of cocaine.[32] Cocaine is processed with chemicals to keep you coming back for more. It causes the user to lie, steal and run through money like a blazing fire in a paper factory.

Bill and Stacy sat waiting in a crowed lobby of St. Johns Mercy Hospital. Nurses and Doctors passed by gazing at their note pads, tending to some patients and overlooking others. Beds were being wheeled to and fro down the long corridors carrying patients that were covered up to their necks with white sheets. Most of them appeared to be injected with IV attachments, either sleep or incoherent from drug doses. Luckily for Bill, he had not encountered any major problems yet. Things were going well from a substance abuse point of view. But, just as things can go well how well it could really go if what you're going for day to day is a chemically dependent reality? Bill sat gaping ahead at the white walls of the hospital, while Stacy covered her face with her hands, crying. Rachael had been rushed to the emergency room. After a night of partying, she had overdosed from an injection of heroin. The doctors were doing everything they could to keep her alive. Bill and Stacy had been at the hospital for more than an hour until finally, a doctor appeared in the waiting room and slowly walked up to Bill. "Are you Mr. Richardson?" "Yes," Bill said. The doctor continued. "I'm sorry, but we will have to notify Rachael's next of kin...she didn't pull through." Stacy let out an agonizing scream and began to sob vehemently. Bill's never ending high with the street girls became a real low. He stepped

---

[32] According to **Servamus,** a South African community-based magazine, the coca plant is the only provider of work for thousands of poor people. Many of these people consider the coca as part of their culture and economical survival. South American civilizations have been chewing cocoa leaves since 3000 BC as a stimulant to work longer and to alleviate the effects of the high altitude, hunger and cold.

back and sat down. Tears began to trickle down his cheeks. He had come to care for Rachael and despite her beaten path, she was a good girl. He fell to his knees and put his head in his hands and in a dramatic call for help, he began to pray out loud… "Oh DEAR GOD! Oh merciful GOD of light and grace…PLEASE let her enter the golden gates of heaven. Raise her spirit and soul up from the darkness of night and dress her in your beautiful white robe and place above her head the halo of righteousness. Let her become an angle in your wonderful kingdom of glory. Shower her with blessings and let her soul rest in peace and her spirit dwell forever. Oh God of Greatness And Love, Please Hear My Prayer!" As if in a trance, Bill stood up and looked around the room appearing to be in search of a miracle. He grabbed Stacy by the hand and they left hospital. There was complete silence in the car as they drove off into the thick, bitter gloom and sadness of the night.

Bill and Stacy drove back to Rachael's home and continued their gripping addition. They squatted there for months, barely keeping up with the expenses until her family was finally able to force them out. They found a vacancy over at the Grand Motel and moved in there. Within a few short weeks, Stacy disappeared into the deep crevices of the crack world… and never came back. Kara had been arrested shortly before Rachael's overdose and was locked up in the Clayton County Jail. These situations sent him back to his mother's house, where she welcomed him in, cautiously but, with open, loving mother's arms. He told his mother he was through with that life, but he continued to use crack and hang out with Rachael's friends. When Kara got out of jail, she and other girl-friends from the street still relied on Bill. He had lost his teaching job with the school district due to drug charges and his arrest. With Rachael not around heading their liaisons, money was tight and he had to take on job assignments through a temp agencies. This was a good thing because it occupied his time, and being preoccupied lessened his use of drugs. He respected his mother enough to not bring it into her house.

One evening, after working all day, Bill was driving home feeling dazed and rather tired. He was a few blocks from his mother's home and he accidentally ran a red light. BOOM…CRASH! He collided with another automobile, badly fracturing his left leg and bruising his face and body. Bill was on his back. Life had knocked him down… for the count. He laid in bed, healing the best he could on his own, and his dear mother did what mother's do. She took care of him while he was debilitated, feeding him and changing his bandages. With care and love, she nursed him back to health. In a couple of months, Bill was able to resume his life, grateful to be alive.

Bill's temp jobs kept him busy and off the streets. He didn't get to spend a lot of time at his mother's house after he recovered from his car accident. He was actively working and grinding trying to get back on the good foot. This particular night, Bill got home and realized his mother wasn't there. He assumed without much thought about it that she was probably at the casino with his auntie, Ann. She had just arrived into town to visit with her sister. Aunt Ann was an adamant gambler with or without company and when she visited the river city, she loved to prance around in the Casinos with her sister.

Bill's cell phone rang. It was his niece Jennifer. The tone of her voice was very distraught and Bill immediately sensed that something was wrong. "I'm at the hospital," she said crying. "Granny had a heart attack and she died, Bill!" Bill dropped the phone from his hands in bewilderment. He was heartbroken. He couldn't believe what he had just heard. Bill's uncle and aunt arrived at his mother's home and drove him to the hospital.

As they made their way up the elevator to where his mother was, the waiting was already filled with her family and friends. Everyone was crying and engulfed with sorrow. He walked into his mother's hospital room and found her lying on the bed cold and lifeless. Bill bent down and tenderly kissed his mother's forehead. He embraced her, not wanting to let go, as if he had been the one who had given life to her. He wept uncontrollably. He then left her side and went into the patient's restroom for privacy. He felt a kind of sorrow and agonizing pain that he was not familiar with. "Who's going to be there for you now?" he thought to himself. There was no love like a mother's love.

Chapter 17

THE DEVIL THAT GOES TO CHURCH

After his mother's passing, Bill continued to reside at his mother's house. He took in his cousin, Keithonian, to help him share the household bills. He thought a lot about the closeness of his family and concluded that this was a good a time to lean on each other. Unlike Bill, his cousin was very religious. He was a practicing Jehovah Witness and frequented the Kingdom Hall constantly engaging himself with religious activities. Shortly into the rooming situation with Keithonian, Bill realized just how often his cousin *wasn't* at the house. He felt good having a roommate to help to pay the bills in these hard economic times, yet it still felt like he lived alone.

Bill continued to hang out with the street girls from time to time. He sought out relief. He was still grief-stricken and needed to keep his mind preoccupied. He thought that he would able to lean on Keithonian, and Keithonian on him, but surprisingly, his cousin bared no compassion over the matter. He revealed an awkward, inverted personality in Bill's presence. It began to make Bill superstitious. He pondered over the superstition, feeling like maybe he had taken in the *devil*. It wasn't long before the two men began to have disputes. Keithonian started displaying deviant acts against Bill. He once circumvented the electricity so that it only operated in his bedroom and not in the rest of the house. Bill felt like he had taken in his cousin with good intentions, and as a result, he was being walked over like a door mat; and it's always the little things that push a person over the edge.

One afternoon, while Bill was sitting in the kitchen repairing his horn, "a little thing" turned into a snapping affair. Bill had recently begun giving saxophone lessons to some of the neighboring students. His angle was to take them to the streets, after their lessons, to play for donations and to hopefully show them the thrills of being a street musician. The sun was shining beautifully outside and Bill wanted to open the door and *Let The Sun Shine In*. His cousin walked in with no regard for the moment

121

and planted himself near where Bill had already set up shop. Bill wasn't in the mood for his awkwardness so he maneuvered around him with no acknowledgment. He needed a small screw driver to work out a problem with his horn. Unable to locate one, he headed to the kitchen drawer for a knife to use instead. "Umm... I'm gonna close this door so flies don't come in," Keithonian said as he got up to shut the door without waiting to hear Bill's reply. It was the **straw that broke the camel's back**. Bill exploded with anger on the inside, but he turned around, looked straight into his cousin's eyes and calmly said, "If you touch that door I'll will pull out a silver cross on you and plunge a stake through your heart." Right before his eyes flashed an animated frightening image of a long green snake camouflaged in tall, green grass. It had a thick, wet, red tongue, resembling a fork that began to rapidly dart in and out of its venomous mouth. It suddenly leaped at Bill sending a gashing flush of shear fear right through him. He shrieked like a white girl from a bad B horror film. The snake looked at him and said, "Don't yell Cousin Bill. Don't yell for heaven's sake... Before you took me in, didn't you know I was a snake?" It slithered away into the tall, green grass....

Later that evening a police officer knocked on Bill's door and ordered him to leave his own home. Keithonian had filed a restraining order against Bill stating that he feared for his life. Bill was given a summons to appear in court and when the time came, he went and he lost. He was given a date to pick up his property and Bill was now officially homeless. What bum luck, he concluded. The street girls came to the rescue and led Bill to the red light district to sleep. On the date ordered by the Judge to pick up his property, Bill went home and noticed his cousin walking down the street. When he yelled out his name, Keithonian kept walking, headed to the Kingdom Hall to pray.

Chapter 18

OUT THERE BAD

Bill fell deeper and deeper into the threaded spider web pathways found in street life. Homelessness combined with the pitfalls of drug addiction had him sleeping in parks, on benches and at bus stops. He had let himself go. Once a responsible productive citizen, Bill had succumbed to the depression of his situation. Instead of the dapper way he used to carry himself before, he now looked rather shabby. He was no longer upstanding and driven. He needed a shave and his clothes were dirty and soiled. It was like he was a refugee in a foreign country waiting on a lift out. The lyrics from a song of the past echoed through his mind, *come on and rescue me.* His life was dreadful, but he rationalized it still feeling like at least he hadn't hit rock bottom yet. It may have looked like the bottom, and he was definitely feeling pretty low, but he knew of no one with a testimony like him that lived to tell about the come up. He was down...but inside, Bill knew he wasn't out. At least, some days he knew this. He picked his horn back up while on the streets and really became a *Street Musician.* He started to frequent the Landing and Riverfront again in an effort to earn money. But, this time it was different. He was different. He was an addict.

One afternoon, while on a mission to score drugs, Bill found himself a more credible place where he could sleep, every night, called The Pallet Yard. It was a trucking business, but the owner permitted the homeless to lodge there providing that they keep the outside area free of trash. It was located in the far north eastern part of St. Louis in a neighborhood where there was a crack house in every block. Even the streets and sidewalks were cracked. It used to be an old German and Irish Immigrant Community during the turn of the nineteenth Century, but now it was about ninety nine percent Black-rented. About one percent of the population there are the original White people who remained with their properties during the massive north side migration of the 60"s. Homes and building were left behind for rent, but over a lengthy period of time, many of them became abandoned or condemned. Large plywood boards cover many windows in the neighborhood. In some sections there are many buildings that are completely abandoned and give the appearance of an Old Wild West Ghost Town. In recent years, some efforts have been made to refurbish parts of the neighborhoods with government housing and private homes for sale.[33]

Looking at the coming together of African and European cultures of music, there is much one can learn regarding race relations. The Blacks and Creoles of New Orleans were forced to live together due to racial segregation. There were so many Creoles of color who resisted the Jim Crow Laws, based on their ancestral heritage. Just to be crystal clear, the courts had to establish a city ordinance, stating that if you were Creole you were henceforth considered to be Black. Nuf said. As a result, the Creoles soon lost their *good* jobs and their perceived social statuses. Many of them had to move in with their "new brothers and sisters." There was a particular neighborhood in the red light district called Storyville where many Black people lived. Storyville was a shanty area that Blacks had come to live in after slavery. It was a place infested with prostitution, crime and gambling. The Creoles who joined the Storyville clan brought their musical education with them to the hood. There were

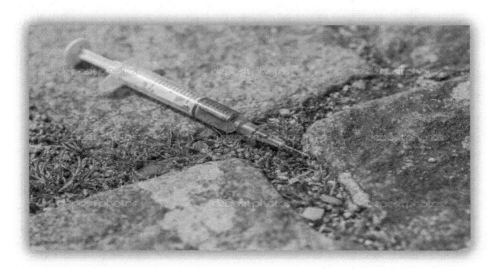

---

[33] There are some Blacks who have taken resident in these beautifully built homes, but the word on the streets is that White folks are slowly moving into these homes to take the city back... Maybe a cultural integration is the key to a better tomorrow.

struggles and cultural differences at the beginning, with the Creoles playing their music soft and politely while the Blacks played their music loud and raw. But, it was this fusion that produced perhaps the greatest and melodious phenomena of our times, jazz music.[34]

The people in Bill's new neighborhood were common folks and lived generally routine lives. Still, Bill dealt exclusively with drug addicts and street girls. The common thread with he and them was the fact that they all smoked crack. They would prow deep into the jungle where lions roared, tigers growled and hyenas laughed for it. Venomous snakes treaded along the tar streets and concrete sidewalks, and Apes swung from tree to tree, all in lay of their prey for that day. Nothing would dissuade them. They were all animals of the jungle and were all well known to bite the hand that fed them. The addicts were a mighty contender in the street jungle, because they had to have it. They took great risk and went to any length to score money for drugs. It was the only real focus they strived for. And none of God's creatures of the jungle could know or challenge the hand of His mighty plan. The wrath of God was the fear of death. However, once you meet Crisscross and Double Cross, you understand that it's a cutthroat game and the wiser creatures of the jungle wore the most vicious of masks. But, still, Bill walked the jungle as a gentle elephant, humble to the nature of humanity. It was GOD's plan that music transform into a golden ticket offering at last a passageway out of the jungle, leading him back into the beauty of this world.

Bill was trying to come up. He had altered his path and had become a full time Street Musician. He wanted to take it more seriously than ever now. He kept himself posted on the major events around town and eventually earned enough money to support himself again. It was an honest hustle. Daily donations from loyal patrons on the busy sidewalks of the Busch Stadium and downtown and the major concerts at the Pageant and at the Scottrade Center; Bill had learned a lot. One thing he did right away was change his aim. Moving forward he sought to mainly cater his music to white audiences. Locally, they were his top contributors and supporters. Tourists were still the best supporters and tippers and of course, when it came to the purest of support, the children

---

[34] *The Encyclopedia of Jazz,* by Leonard Feathers

were at the top of the list. Bill loved the genuineness of their appreciation. He recalled the many occasions where he had to play in the raw, or when he would get to an event late, or having to start his day with his horn wedged between his lips *Smack Dab In The Middle* of a crowd of people with no time for preparation. He relied heavily on spontaneity. He played just to get the people to laugh and dance; to get couples to embrace during a song of romance.

Some people applauded Bill's choice to be a street musician. They respected the idea of enjoying what you're doing, making it appear easy and getting paid for it. When they came, he would accept the compliments with a smile and talk to the friendlier people for a while. He had to work up a system though. He would chat it up for a short while and then he would eventually focus his attention back on playing his horn, because on the real, he knew there was nothing easy about making money. Making money may seem easy by some who have simplified their method, but money was nothing to play with, except when you take it to the casino. It was his experiences playing out at casinos that made him realize where he should focus his energy. The crowds are mostly Black people and everybody knows, Black people don't tip. Donations were far and few. He could understand the lack of donations from the people who gambled at the casino all the time cause most of them were broke when they got there and even more so when they left. One lady leaving the casino even stopped in front of Bill and asked him for five dollars. When he gave it to her, she turned around and went back into the casino.

Bill sat at the Landing one late afternoon playing his saxophone for donations. A man walked his way, put some change into his bag and asked him to play a particular song by The Five Heart Beats. Bill told him that he didn't know that particular song, but could ask if he could play another one instead. The man asked him for his money back. Reluctantly Bill reached into his bag and gave the man a dollar bill. The man had the nerve to stand there in front of Bill attempting to explain himself. He was so drunk and busted; Bill could not understand what he was saying. The man was licking on a sucker and told Bill his name was Timothy Tucker. He plucked from his pucker the sucker he had been licking, and with his red tongue flicking a click and clucker and looked at Bill and called him a motherfucker. "Move on along, man," Bill was done.

It was a slow afternoon of donations, so Bill called it. He still had plans to work an event later that evening at the Fox Theater. As he packed up, a young man showed up hoping to catch the street musician in action. "Darn! You're all packed up and ready to leave," the man said. "My friends and I are from out of town and we have been enjoying your music very much, you know the little we heard." He handed Bill a twenty dollar bill. "Would you mind playing a little longer?" The man went back to his table to join his friends and Bill obliged the young crowd of listeners. He stayed and played for thirty more minutes. While he blew his horn, two young women came dancing down the cobble stone street. They were scantily dressed leaving hardly anything at all to Bill's imagination. His eyes were feeling glorious and delightful at the slightly treat. His senses began tingle as their bodies went jingle, jingle, jingle in rhythmic undulation.

"Hey sax man," one of the women said. "Play something romantic for us by Billie Holiday." Bill was surprised at the woman's request. It showed that she knew a thing or two about good music. He played Good Morning Heartache for the ladies and they just stood there beside him, listening with amazement. The whistled and clapped with approval and cheer at the song's end. They were from Farmington, Missouri and promised to come looking for Bill the next time they came back to St. Louis. They both dropped in their donations for him along with a wink and a smile. This turned out to be a best thirty minutes of the gig day, Bill thought as he began to take apart his saxophone for the second time. Another woman, out of nowhere, appeared in front of him. "You're not going anywhere," she said. "Stay right here and play that saxophone some more! Your music makes people so happy...we can feel the love when you blow." She looked him in the eyes. "I'm not sure if you realize this, but it's true. It touches hearts and fills the atmosphere with so much beauty." She handed Bill a donation and he again put his horn back together and sat down and played. Bill was touched and felt sort of a confirmation of his plight. Bill was passionately playing, unaware of his complete surroundings. The next time he looked up for the woman, she had gone. He wanted to give the donation back to her because the words she conveyed to him were worth more than money. She quickly and deeply affected him. Her compliments came from a place of Selflessness,[35] a type of admiration and that is a rarity these days. Bill appreciated this very much because to give love and get love in return is the greatest thing in life.[36] This really was indeed the highlight of his afternoon.

Bill made his way back home to the Pallet Yard. He tried to be as generous as possible to his neighbors. The women on the yard were not his type. The ones that he associated with weren't worth two dead flies, but he treated them nice and with respect A sense of fairness has always been one of his attributes; treat others as you want them to treat you. However, he quickly learned that dealing with the golden rule in a crowd that does not play fair was very difficult and frustrating and he vowed to maintain his attributes and sense of standards. He out right refused to adapt to the behavior and values of the people he associated with. *The truth* and *a lie* meant the same thing to them. They would manipulate and edit either to fit their needs. Trickery and deception among them was okay. How can they have respect for you? Rehabilitation has good qualities and works for some, but how can someone go back to using a value system that they have never had. They may know of a better value system, but they could be discouraged from using it in their environment. We all want to live a good life, but no one is perfect. Human beings are prone to make seventeen mistakes a day if only in their thought patterns.[37] Bill encountered many trying times, some of which almost made him do some really stupid shit. His nature of kindness was taken advantage of over and over, but he did not bend or break. Bill was aware that most of the people he dealt with were not compassionate. The instinctual nature of survival can lead a person to commit some very unpleasant behaviors. Self-preservation is also a natural human inclination[38]. Giving these matters very thoughtful consideration, miraculously Bill managed to stay strong adhering to his nature and adhering to the GOD given spirit that guided him through the treacherous jungle of the Hood.

Bill was intrigued with the respectful nature of the Chinese people and felt that we as Americans could learn something from them. He had

---

[35] *The Best of John Coltrane*, Album John Coltrane

[36] A song titled *Nature Boy,* by Nat KING Cole

[37] A book titled *Tolstoy* by Leo Tolstoy

[38] *The Virtue of Selfishness* by Ayn Rand

been reading publications about their culture, and he had had encounters with a few of them on the streets, and was impressed with their capability for kindheartedness. China has the largest population in the world with over 1.3 billion people; a host of congeniality! They always seem to present themselves with such an outstanding persona of human compassion and that's an extremely large number of people practicing behaviors that are genuinely nice, decent, and humble to their blessings. It's something to be admired. Many Christians say they follow the teachings of Jesus Christ; teachings similar to, but greater than the acts of kindness displayed by the Chinese culture in which Bill looked up to. But, anyone will tell you that if you say the wrong thing to them at the wrong time, or even disagree with them, you will get cut, or stabbed...no, SHOT! Very often Bill would say that the music was in his left hand and a bible was in his right hand. He believed in the Son of GOD, Jesus, as many cultures around the globe do; every race and religion presenting their own "version" of his image. But, GOD never revealed to man his image, so we have no concept of what his image could be. Many biblical notations hail Jesus as the greatest human being to have walked this earth. Bill always said, "Moses has got my back," and he would say that Jesus walked ahead of him paving the way for him...leaving footprints in the grimy dirt for him to follow. The times when he felt defeated, like no one cared, and wanted to just throw up both his hands, he resolved that he was just being carried through... from there only being one set of footprints imprinted in the dirt. He continued to wish for better days.

Bill talked to a few people, but for the most part he kept to himself in the Yard. Still, whenever he made a drug score, the addicts would come scurrying out of their trailers with the anticipation of getting a free hit. On many occasions his trailer would become a party house. When Bill came on the scene, Christmas trees would light up. He met a fellow 'Yarder'; people called him Double E. Double E. would wake up in the mornings with crack on his mind. He'd come by Bill's spot, early, and they would sit and smoke crack until it was all gone. Then, Double E would go and get more of it and they would continue to smoke. He was a professional thief and he stole a lot of CBs. He kept a host of CB radios and equipment in the back seat and trunk of his new Grand AM. He used the doors of his car to advertise the CBs to truck drivers. Despite the fact that he was a criminal, Bill considered him respectful and thought he treated people fair. But, one unfaithful day for Double E, he got himself caught with a trunk full of CB radios. He was arrested and sent away to do hard time.

Bill also befriended a pair of identical twin sisters who knew the streets as well as they knew each other. Bill learned early on not to offer solutions for the two sisters during disputes because they both would drop their disputes and turn on him. First, there was Lil' Baby. She was a perilous female gangster and she didn't take shit from anyone, especially men. And she could take down a man too. Many tall tales floated around the neighborhood about her. Big Baby was the treacherous one, clever and very swift with the sleight of hand.

When Bill first hung out with them, the three of them were going to make a score. Big Baby took the back seat of Lil' Baby's car and Bill was in the front seat. Big Baby asked Bill for a cigarette and a light. He gave her a cigarette and his red lighter but then couldn't find his pack of Kool Blues to put back into his pocket. He brushed if off, figuring he dropped the pack in between the seats and would find it after they returned. After they reached their destination, Bill couldn't find his money. As he searched his pockets over and over Big Baby impatiently jumped out of the car and went into the crack house. By the time Lil Baby fully parked and turned off the car, Big Baby and the dope man were coming out the front door. The drug dealer yelled out, "It's all bad. She cleaned me out." Big Baby had bought the entire package. he didn't even consider her sister or Bill. She planned to break it down and re-sell it. But, everyone on the block knew that if they bought from her, the first rock she sells you would be good, but that second rock would be a balled up piece of white gum or some other serious dummy look-a-like. Lil' Baby wasn't having any of it and she insisted that her sister either hand over half the package or get put out of the car. Bill stayed out of the quarrel. It was a long walk home and three o'clock in the morning, so Big Baby grudgingly backed down. She halfheartedly divided the package and handed half to her sister. Then, Lil' Baby pulled off as Bill watched Big Baby take out a cigarette from a package of Kool Blues and light it with a red lighter.

Chapter 19

THE JOURNEY TO RECOVERY

Bill walked the streets of the Hood every day. Some days he had to stand in a food line to eat. There were Church people who drove around in trucks on some days that provided fresh clothing and food for the homeless. Bill was grateful for the opportunity to play at the baseball games, but the games were getting old. Bill's life wasn't going anywhere. Every morning he would wake up broke because the night before all of this money that he had worked so hard to make went up in smoke. He felt it was time to look into finding a drug abuse treatment facility. He began attempts to curtail his drug habit, but he kept walking down the same ole cracked streets and falling on the same ole sidewalk cracks with some ole crack! He just couldn't get right…not continuing on the same path that he had been on. His sole solution was to change his surroundings. He woke up one morning and volunteered himself to a drug treatment facility. It was hard, and the road backwards was tempting, but Bill kept his focus on recovery. At the treatment facility is where Bill found a new voice. He began to write, and his mind became very clear, focused and eventually free of drugs.

After graduating from the drug treatment facility Bill was placed in a live-in Residential Treatment Center to help adjust back into the world he has to live in. One night while in his room he got down on his knees and asked GOD for forgiveness from his love ones whom his drug addiction had affected. Only now could he realize how miserable his addiction must have made their lives. Addiction involves a defect in someone's personality and may never go away. It creates greediness within and the only cure is to feed the urge by any means necessary. Understanding the nature of the beast, Bill cautiously forged ahead avoiding the triggers that may wake the sleeping beast up.

Shortly after Bill began to mend his life back together he was diagnosed with cancer. This news devastated him and he became overwhelmed with depression. Overcoming his dependency on drugs was a struggle in and of itself, but now he has cancer to work into the equation. Bill knew he had to be strong and fight through this newest wave of unfortunate luck. From the options his doctors had given him, Bill chose to have surgery. There were long months of suffering and stress that he had to bear, but after the surgery, the cancer went into remission. While this was great news for Bill, he still continued to experience the effects of his disease, suffering through months of agonizing physical pain. He continued to work through his dismal feelings, determined to stride forward with relentless focus. He spent a great deal of his rejuvenated moments writing. He wrote down his thoughts, poems, lyrics, raps and music for songs. Bill felt himself becoming something else. He was a musician who now aspired to be an author. It just so happened that the Residential home provided regularly scheduled computer classes and proficient instructors who equipped him with the skills on how to turn his writings into computerized book materials.

Over the many months in the Residential home Bill began to heal more and more. He also began practicing his saxophone again. He started making those familiar trips again, around the city and downtown area, and to the hockey and football games, with horn in bag on back. Things were finally coming into place for him and he began to make a living again as a *Street Musician*. He felt good to have yesterday's money still in his pocket. Bill was back.

Chapter 20

MANHATTAN

Downtown Manhattan was much different from Marlys' hometown of St. Louis. She had at last made it to New York City, and she couldn't be more excited. It was the most popular and the most unique city in the United States to her! It just seemed to have a culture all its own. She dreamed of going since she was a little girl, but never made until now. Luckily for her, she came because she was the *Queen*. Marlys was scheduled to perform at the famous Apollo Theater in New York. She was booked as one of the headliners for a benefit concert hosted by Live Aid to help the city's homeless population, particularly families and mothers with children who had no place to live. Concerts of this nature always leave everyone involved feeling like they have done a good deed, being a part of such a large pool of giving. It also obviously helps the intended group of people who will receive the aid money. It was a new charity so Marlys was happy that this charity could continue to raise money even after the concert was over. When she sang, she sang from her soul, and she was elated to hear that the show was already sold out. She had never been able to separate music from life and that's what made this concert so wonderful.

Marlys couldn't soak up all the sights of the city, because in a couple of days she was scheduled to be on a plane headed to Hollywood, California. Her agent called and told her she just got booked to perform on the Barry Hathaway show. But, today she was in New York and it was a special day for her. Today she was performing in a big concert with other great and famous artists for an amazing and worthy cause; she even heard that the famous star Beyoncé Knowles may end up making an appearance. This was an important show for her because this show could lead to more concerts and tours.

While in the big apple Marlys also scheduled a recording session for her new upcoming CD with a local producer in New York named Ruben. She had spent months working on her new album and there was one song that she wrote that required a certain sound and production. She tried out a few of the producers in St. Louis that she works with, but hadn't heard any tracks that she felt fit the context of this song. Ruben was an old college friend who was a very popular and well respected producer in NYC. He had been writing for many of the big named recording artists for years and had made a great living with his talent. He wasn't cheap either. He was one of the more expensive producers in the city, but his tracks were well worth it. Ruben had produced the perfect track for her song and she was ready to blend the lyrics with the music. She was hoping that this tune would be as catchy and captivating as her first recording was. Her new CD would be titled, *Come Hip Hop with Me.*

The show at the Apollo went on without a hitch and the thrill of success bubbled all through the new star. She woke up still feeling the rush of last night's show. No doubt she gained a slew of new fans. Day two in Manhattan; she had a lot of things to squeeze in such a short visit. There was a jazz joint called The *Village Vanguard* that she wanted to go to. She had heard that many musicians referred to it as the "Carnegie Hall of Jazz." It was said to be one of the more serious jazz clubs in the city. Although she wanted to go, there was no time for it. All she had time for were her two previously scheduled events. She had an appointment with a New York fashion designer who had designed some new costumes for her to try on. She was excited because she had some ideas she wanted to talk with him about regarding a new design for the golden crown she wore on her head when she performed.

Marlys gazed out of her hotel window at the lustrous city. She was wearing an attractive red cotton ensemble with a very short fitting skirt that left her sexy thighs revealed to one's imagination. Around her neck she wore a diamond necklace and a matching diamond bracelet on her thin wrist. She was wearing heels that reflected like glass. She dabbed on to her neck her newest favorite sweetly scented perfume from Clive Christian and glanced into the tall full-length mirror. She felt absolutely gorgeous and ready to step out into the sleepless city. First on her things to do in New York was her lunch date and studio session Ruben. She noticed the time. It was almost noon! He would be calling for her at any moment. Suddenly, the expected phone call came. A hotel escort was on his way up to her suite to join her with her guest.

Chapter 21

HE MUST HAVE BEEN AN ANGEL

Since there was no baseball game at the stadium, Tommy was working security at the Scottrade Center. He noticed Bill working on his instrument. He knew something was wrong with it because he didn't hear him playing. He had just arrived to work and was running a little behind schedule so he didn't stop to chit and chat. By the time he made it back outside to check on him, Bill was gone.

He woke up the next morning with an idea. He would stop by Bill's apartment to see if he could help. It was 10 am when Tommy knocked on the door. Bill was still in the bed, but he got up and opened the door. Surprised, Bill smiled and asked, "Tommy? What brings you by here so early?" "Get your saxophone and come with me," he said. "Where are we going", Bill asked. "I'll let that be a surprise," he responded. Bill quickly brushed his teeth and hair, freshening up a bit, and slipped into his clothing. He grabbed his saxophone, and followed Tommy down the stairs to his car.

While they were riding, Bill said to Tommy, "My saxophone is not working." "I know", Tommy said. "I saw you at the Scottrade Center last night. I came by to shoot the shit for a bit with you after handling some business I had to address inside, but you had left. A musician that plays as well as you play needs a saxophone that works." They pulled up to Baton Music Store located on Delmar Boulevard in the U-City Loop. Tommy parked his car in front of the store and they went in. Tommy appeared to know the owner as they greeted each other and shook hands. "This is Bill, the musician I was telling you about. He has a saxophone that's in need of repair, or maybe he can trade it in for one that works." The owner asked Bill if he could take a look at his saxophone. Bill took it from the duffle bag and handed it over to him. The owner agreed that it was indeed in need of repair. He could see the rubber bands stretching along the surface. He looked very closely at the name brand on Bill's horn and said, "You see those Saxophones over there in that cabinet behind you? Select one from there. We can make an even swap at no cost ." Bill turned and looked with amazement at the shiny new saxophones. They were used, but they were in great condition, especially compared to the ole faithful one he had been blowing for years. He blew into one after the other until he found one that had the sound and feel that satisfied him. He turned to the owner and said, "I like this one." And just like that, the owner handed Bill a store receipt for ownership. Bill thanked him and Tommy and promised the owner that he would come back and play in front of his store to show his appreciation and show off the quality of instruments that were being sold there. The owner smiled and stated that he would be honored.

Bill and Tommy left the store and went into a nearby bar for a drink. Bill felt like celebrating. Bill was very elated at what had just transpired. They cheered it up with shots of Bill's favorite whisky while engaging in conversations with two young ladies they just met inside the bar. After throwing a few back, Tommy drove Bill back downtown to his apartment. Bill thanked Tommy again. At this point Tommy was certainly a real friend to Bill and someone who had proven to genuinely care. Bill was relieved and felt blessed to have that type of ally on his team. They made it back to Bill's place and Bill and Tommy said their goodbyes. Bill rushed up the stairs to his apartment and immediately began to play his new saxophone.

Chapter 22

CHICAGO IS IN TOWN

The Cardinals were in town for a home game with the Cubs. They had already played two games and this third game would break the tie. Fans and vendors swarmed the sidewalks and streets buying and selling souvenirs. Many people in the streets rooting for the Cardinals, danced around in high spirits flaunting memorabilia and passing out leaflets. The streets were also filled with street musicians. Chicago horn players along with St. Louis horn players were on the corners belching out good music to the fans. One player from Chicago came on the corner where Bill was playing talking about "man, this is my turf!" Bill was almost tickled. "I've been playing on this corner since the beginning of the year. Plus I live here...all of this, I got first dibs on." "Well, not today," the belligerent Chicagoan argued. "I'm playing here today. Now, what do you have to say about that?" Bill allowed himself to engage in an argument with the man over the mater. "If you think you're Al Capone because you're from Chicago, then guess what? I'm motherfuckin J. Edger Hover of the F.B.I." At that moment, Officer Tommy appeared and approached the Chicago player. "Do you have a street permit sir?" The player responded, "No. I left it at home by accident." "Then you will have to leave," Tommy said. "He (referring to Bill) didn't show me his permit," the Chicago player exclaimed. "He doesn't have to because you are not a police officer. Politely remove yourself from around here; and if I catch you down here playing without a permit, you will get locked up." At the mention of being locked up, the Chicago musician turned around and left. Enough said.

Bill sat at the corner of 8th Street and Clark Street playing his saxophone to the passersby. All of a sudden, there was a big roar coming from the Stadium. People began yelling out that the Cardinals had won. As the crowd poured out from the Stadium, Bill blew his horn in merriment. He too was a big Cardinal fan. He also couldn't help thinking about the bigger picture. The better the Cards do, the more it attracts tourists to the city; and the more tourists that come into the city, the greater the opportunity is for Bill to make more of them *dollar dollar bills*. He played the Martha Reeves hit song, *Dancing In The Street*. After all, that is exactly what the people were doing, parting in the streets. Everyone was in high spirits. There were strangers hugging strangers. Even the Cubs fans couldn't escape the love. Bill then started to play a funky patriotic song, *Living In America*, by James Brown! Bill played and played and it seemed like the excitement would never end, but eventually it did. His bag of donations was filled to the brim. It had been a good day for the Cardinals and for 'Dollar Bill'. The day didn't go so well, however, for the Chicago Cubs or for at least one of the Chicago street musicians. Oh Well...Peace Out Chicago!

Chapter 23

THE HOMELESS

A week had passed since the Cardinals won the tie breaker game against Chicago. Bill set up at Kiener Plaza to play his saxophone. The homeless began to gather around him, enjoying the sounds of the *Music Man*. Bill had songs just for them. You see, he played to the natural pulse and resonance of the streets. To him, there were no prejudices in music. Music didn't care if you lived in a mansion or under a cardboard box. It freely flowed like water and poured through every crevice and hole in humanity. It offered up inspiration and it opens up the soul. Bill had come to realize this over time. This is really why he chose to be a street musician. He himself was homeless for a period of time in his life and hope and inspiration was hard to find. Music fills that need for free.

The St. Louis homeless population lived among the rhythms and sounds of the streets, in dilapidated and condemned vacant buildings. They inhabited the dwellings of Catholic Charities, the courthouses, the public libraries, park benches, and any shelters with a room available. Wherever they ended up for the night, they were back on the streets at 5 am with nowhere to be. They hung out in alley ways; they laid out on the concrete, brick and asphalt grounds; they raided trash bends and garbage cans and they even escaped into the round metal sewage tops and manholes. A popular place for them to settle was at the bus and Metro Link stops, or places where they could keep warm, like sidewalks where vents blew out hot air. They were slow moving members of our society with no particular place to go. They would stop strangers, begging them for money to get something to eat, and when begging wasn't enough they became diggers, digging into trash bins to collect soda cans. None of them were able to hold down a job. Their future was grim to say the least. Adapting to the compelling laws of street life was no easy feat, especially when it appears that you can never escape from it. Standing in the dark, bleak shadows and feeling the deep pain of hunger and the agony of defeat, taking chances and going to jail, all in an effort to survive another day. Destitution even stifled their need for love. They often wondered if anyone care or if their loved ones knew they were out there bad like that. They wondered if life would ever get any better for them. Some still had at least an ounce of their pride and appeared tough, coming off bitter, holding back silent tears while living in desperation, humiliation and dehumanization. Integrity, dignity and pride were not on their side; those things can't be used when you have holes in your shoes. When all that you own is hanging on your back, falling down is no big whop because the homeless life is surrounded by hopelessness. But, what doesn't kill you makes you stronger, they say. These were the rhythms and sounds of street music.

Bill played from his heart and soul, out into a wide and open space of the park, where motorists and pedestrians walking by noticed him, not just the homeless. They stopped or paused and turned their heads in curiosity to look, with an appreciative smile of delight. That day, Bill didn't play any cover songs. Everything he played was purely off the cuff. He improvised with a spirit of vibrancy and spontaneity.

He received no more than a hand full of coins in donations, which was more than he expected. He did just play for a bunch of homeless people.

What did they have to give? They definitely didn't have any money. Yet, he still ended up with some change in his bag. The one thing they did have was love for the *Music Man* and that's what they gave. After Bill ended every tune he played, the group of derelict listeners screamed and clapped, very loudly causing Bill to blush over and over again. The love they shared with Bill caused Bill to, by default, give them what they wanted right back. Everyone has a need to be wanted and they had an unalienable right to enjoy their life.

After a few hours, Bill packed up his instrument to go to his next destination. Someone from the crowd yelled out to him, "Hey Music Man, where are you going?" Bill responded with the biggest smile they had seen on him all afternoon, "The Queen of Venus is performing!" He slung his duffel bag over his shoulder and exited the park.

Chapter 24

WE MEET AGAIN

People were all over the Stadium grounds. There were venues and tents scattered ever where. At the Club Paddy 'O there was an outside stage set up. The Queen of Venus had contracted an agreement to make an appearance with her old group The Bright Stars. The show was more a gesture to show her appreciation for them. It was like a reunion. It was promised to be one of the best shows of the year. The fans filled the grounds and Bill was one of them.

The Queen of Venus sat in her limousine waiting to be ushered into the club by her entourage of escorts. Once inside the club, she joined her group members in preparation for show. She spoke with the production manager and found out that there was a discrepancy in being paid for the show as specified in the contract. It seems that the business office of Spot Light Entertainment, the company that hired her, made an error. The check that she was expecting to receive before the show had yet to be drawn up. When the production manager witnessed the reaction that the Queen gave them to the news about her money not being ready, doubt and skepticism filled the air. Everyone began to wonder whether or not the group would perform. The business manager apologized to everyone for the error and then he looked at the Queen and promised her that she would receive payment when the office opened first thing Monday morning. That solution didn't satisfy her one bit. The manager begged and pleaded with her not to back out of the gig, continuing to make promises to her. This time he promised to pull a few strings and get the check to her immediately after the show. Although she knew it was a gamble to not go by the terms of the contract, the sounds of the roaring fans began to pull at her heartstrings. The last thing she wanted was to ever do was disappoint the fans, so she agreed to perform.

The crowd outside became nearly restless as they waited for the show to began. "We want the Queen of Venus! We want the Queen of Venus", they chanted. Bill was right up front near the entry where The Queen and The Bright Stars would be coming up to the stage. "Bill," someone shouted out from behind. Bill was so excited about the show that it took him a few seconds to react to the fact that someone could be calling out to *him*. After all, Bill is a pretty common name. When he turned around and looked out into the audience he didn't recognize anyone that he knew right off the bat. He did see that there was a guy looking at him, smiling. Bill thought he may know him from playing out on the streets. "Hey Music Man, where is that sax? Play for us man, play for us!" Bill didn't pull out his sax to play it, but he smiled.

A spokesman from Spot Entertainment appeared on stage and announced that there was a small delay in the scheduled performance. "If everyone would bare a little patience, the show would go on momentarily." The crowded booed at the announcement as the spokesperson left the stage. They continued to yell, "We want the Queen of Venus! We want the Queen of Venus." At that moment, Bill decided to take out his sax. He walked onto the stage in front of a microphone. He blew a couple of notes to test the sound. The crowd cheered and began to shout, "Play that horn! Play that horn!" The microphone carried the sound of his horn all over the tented area. The sun reflected onto his shiny instrument with a radiance of glitter and gold. He began to play a funky melody. Then, out of the blue, other people began to climb onto the stage. They were the homeless people he played for at the Kiener Plaza. They grabbed the microphones and began to rap to rhythm. Some of them beat on their chest into the microphones. It reflected the sound of a bass drum. They made sounds with their mouth that emulated percussive instruments. Bill had a rhythm section. It was amazing! The people were fascinated with their demonstrations of talent. The huge crowd of people began to calm down and dance.

The Queen of Venus looked through the window and was also amazed at what was going down on the stage. Right away, she wanted to know who the man was playing the saxophone. She had heard that saxophone before. None of her group members knew who the sax player was either, but she was determined to find out. Then, it came to her suddenly out of the blue. She thought could this be Bill, the Street Musician?

She quickly walked out the club and treaded through the crowd and onto the stage. Her group shortly followed. The homeless people exited the stage as an announcer came up to the microphone. Bill gathered his belongings and stepped off to the side of the stage. "Ladies and gentleman…I hope you're ready! Help me welcome to the stage these Lovely Ladies of the Lou… The Bright Stars!" The crowd applauded as The Bright Stars went up to the front of the stage. The Queen grabbed Bill by the arm and said to him, "Wait! I want you stay and play that sax." They had a few minutes before it was time for her to come to the stage. Bill took the time to try and quickly expressed his love for her music and his appreciation for this impromptu opportunity. She smiled a smile that seemed reached around the crowd and right back to Bill. The crowd roared as they announced The Queen Of Venus to the stage. She turned to Bill and said, "Come On!!" He followed her onto the stage and found a place to blow. He played to her songs and embellished them with his horn spontaneously, taking solos where he could fit it in. He played the entire show with the Queen of Venus, the famous hip hop star.

The show was over, but the party didn't stop. Bill grabbed his duffel bag of donations from the edge of the stage. "You won't need that bag anymore," the Queen said as she took her spark of crown and placed it on Bill's head. "You're in my band now." She kissed his cheek and the crown tumbled off his head. He quickly caught it and they burst into laughter. "Make sure it's on tight this time if you're going to dance with me." They could hear the sounds of another street musician playing to the dwindling crowd. She began to whisper a romantic song into Bill's lending ear as they slowly danced in each other's arms, backstage, in a warm, passionate embrace. Fate manifested a beautiful beginning.

The Magic Of Love

It's that time again to say goodbye to a friend
We join hands in the dark
Found romance in the sunshine above
And I don't really want to say goodbye
I feel the magic of love

There have been so many who've let me down
Broken dreams is all I found
So now when they get too close
I pack up and slip away, but this time
I want to stay... I feel the magic of love

'Cause babe when I'm with you
I feel the magic of love
And when the sun comes shinning through
I feel the magic of love
And when you say you love me too
I feel the magic of love

You say good-bye to love and new love starts
Still there's pain in your heart
But all the good that love has done
There's somebody of everyone
And since I met you babe
I feel the magic of love

THE END

APENDIX

The music celebrities and stars of today hold the power to make improvement in music's contributions to American society. The message is loud and clear: (1) it's time to take responsibility for actions; the affect that music generates on the young population, (2) transcend from the lifestyle of the Hood, (3) take music to a higher level of affect where it positively influences the world. For, we are merely puppets in a society that generates greed and peril and future generations will reap from the demanding, detrimental fruits of lust and pleasure. A puzzle is not complete until it's been fulfilled with all of its symmetrical pieces in proper placement. Part of the truth is a lie. But, we must face the music one day. You can fill your life with trickery and deceit, but you can't win with a lie, and you can't hide from the truth forever.

You can run from American Justice, but you cannot run from the Holy Justice that has been placed here by a Higher Power to guide us through our lives from beginning to end. Music speaks the truth as it blares out of our TV's, radios, CD players, universal speakers, voices, computers, laptops, tablets, iPods and pads, door bells, cell phones, alarm clocks, tiny toys for children, churches, dives, back alleyways, street corners, office intercoms, speeding trains, elevators, motorcycles and speed boats. We listen to music when we race along in our trucks vans or cars. We can hear music at the top of the Gateway Arch! We sleep with its comfort and wake up to its broadcast of news. We dance with laughter to its rhythm. We embrace it with love. It's magic. It's a medicine. It's a healer.

Voice is the very first instrument to produce music by man. It's GOD given. Music is an expression of human emotions. Manufactured musical instruments are meant to imitate the voice. The first man made instrument, the drum, was used extensively in Africa to make music to where the voice could not reach. Some musical instruments have surpassed the technical ability of the voice, but they cannot

146

exceed the human quality of the voice, which is an essential element of music. When there is a voice among a group of instruments, it normally dominates the ensemble, whether it is background or lead. The instruments are used to assist the voice. We can readily relate to a voice singing in a language that we understand. We immediately get the message loud and clear.

Studies have discovered that all of the muscles in the entire body go weak when, for example, subjected to the irregular beats in rock music, calling it a "switching" of the brain; which occurs when the actual symmetry between both of the cerebral hemispheres are destroyed causing alarm in the body, lessened work performance, learning and behavior problems in children, and a general depression in adults.[39] So, playing the "wrong note" can do more than just affect our ears in an unpleasant way. Correspondingly, making wrong life decisions leads to negative results. Greed can lead a person to take detrimental actions against another. Violence and disrespect can be unpleasant and usually leads to aggregated circumstances and complications. Why is there a need to kindle a fire in a society that's about to explode from what has been fed and recycled through its system. This is not the work of GOD.

Lucifer, the angel of hell, has been said to have been kicked out of heaven because he took advantage of the seductive quality music produces, and used to it to entice wondering souls to execute his evil deeds. Music is from heaven and should be used to assist the positive creation of life, not destroy it.

Music is a tool of communication, a language. The Federal Government categorizes the mandated rules and regulation of music under the Freedom of Speech Constitutional Amendment.

---

[39] Australian physician and psychiatrist, Dr. John Diamond, *The Life Energy In Music: Three Volume Series*

The most influential Continent in music is Africa. The most popular music in the world is the music created in America. The foundation of American music is built on the foundation of voice. As slaves, the Black Americans resentfully sang to accommodate those woes as they were forced to work the toiling tasks that help build this country. Every musical innovation in this country has been produced by Black Americans. American music may seem to be unique, but it is undeniably a variation of music form that has ventured around the world for thousands of years recording the history, culture, and realities of human existence, and street music.

When the Sun First Bloomed A Golden Flower
Shedding Shafts Of Warm Light And Yellow
Shower Through The Blackness Of Space
With No Given Aim... Then Westering In A
Golden Red Flame And The Moon Stood High
Like A Bright White Dove Clothing The Night
With Its Soft Pearly Light Like A Fleece And The
Distant Stars That You Now See Glowed Like
The Glitter Of Crystal Jewelry... White Pillowing
Clouds Filled The Air Like Flocks Of Wild Geese
When The Skies Were Pure And Deep Blue
Misted, From The Earth Flowed Freely A
Red Belching Liquid Before The Pendulum
Of Time Began To Sweep For
Earthly Creatures Was There Not Peace

The Street Musician

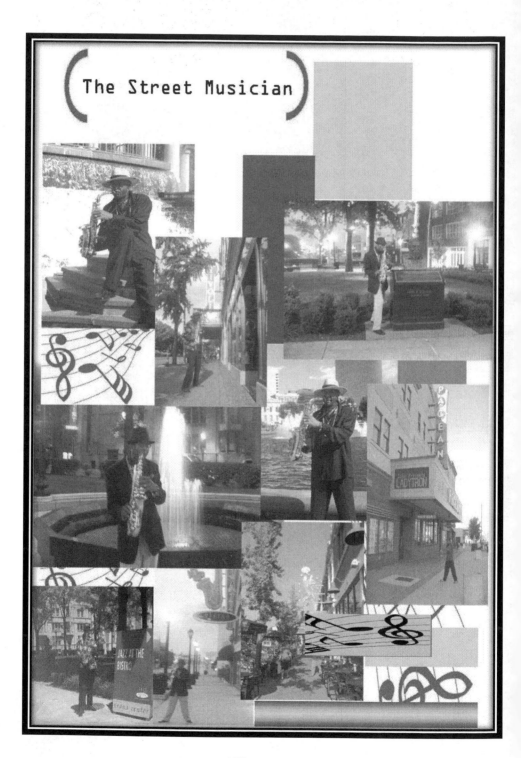

152

ONE HOT SUMMER NIGHT

One hot summer night on a damp bed of green

I opened my eyes as I rose from a dream…

There was a dazzling figure high above my head

Against a darkened sky of blue scorched with rustic red.

A beautiful woman danced among the glitter of stars

Bouncing and wiggling her hips around

To the melodious sound

Of the rhapsodically drone of a saxophone…

Her head of dress was like a window display

Fashioning a four corner star pointed jewel crown

Of yellow gold with blotches of blue and white sapphire

Gleaming over a splendor of radiant wine and red rocks

Of rubies that entwined it in a circular motion of bound

Like a merry go round with glistening diamond lacings

That spun and twirled onto winding beaded poles of

Solid white pearls with a dispersion of many

Shades of gems and shining trinkets that cropped the top

Of dome and clung to the sides like spinning rims

With projection of an hypnotic reflection

From the bouncing of motion as she moved and grooved

To the sound of the saxophone...

Her hair bore the colors of autumn leaves that hung

Like dangling thick threads of decoratively woven

Flowers that blossomed into clusters of petals

And eloquent curls falling along her sleek of neck

Spilling onto her deep sensuous cleavage of nest

And bosomed into a white soft purple gown of breast

That hung down to her small of feet of

Glowing silver slippers with cushioned comfort soles

That reflected like mirror glass

When she walked the guardian paths

Of heaven's treasure map of golden brick roads.

The silver light of moon gave sparkle to

The golden crystal dust of magic sand she blew softly

From her exquisitely thin, white glove of hand...

Which came down from above like a golden

Milk of love spreading onto the shrine of stars that spiral

The planets like a galaxy around Saturn, Venus,

Jupiter and Mars... Like falling drops of rain and wind

That stirs the bush of grass and trees of earthly plains

Of browns and greens, forming a rainbow cloud

Of mystic vaporance around my dome like

Skull of mesmerance...I drank onto a breath of thee

And as the misty puff of cloudy smoke

Filled to the deepest cavity of my mouth and throat

The music from the saxophone that excited her,

So enchanted me until I shivered rocked shook

And then rolled from the sensationalized tingling

Of my body from the bottom to the top

To the deepest cavity of my very soul....

I went to shout a call of name of which I did not know

So I gave a savage cry of me through tears of fears

Of unknown emotions as apprehension soon dissolved into

an oblivious state of distortion Onto a tenaciously

driven course ... A powerful mental force.

An undefined moment of existence where I relinquished

Surrender to the Unrelenting agony from a most

Enjoyable pain and blissful pleasures of a

Pulsating climatic delight of delicacy

Derived from the total thrill of ecstasy ...

She quickly turned her head, like a dervish

Towards me and whispered an unpretentious

Kiss in my direction from traceable lips

Painted of dark maroon with a face of

Tenderness ripened with passionate affection

Her skin was like a soft rich caramel candy

Of tangy brown sweet tasting tootsie taffy

Of golden honey suckle Thick of sappy

Her seducing eyes shimmered bright like a cat of night

With flashing designer shadowed eyes of lashes

Lined with red black and blue colors of fashion

She was enticing me with winks and beckoning me

With a flexing of a finger call of questing

with a promise of forever love...

She moved with the gracefulness of a gazelle and

The royalty and eloquence of a Princess of heritage

Through descended fine quality of Generations of

Angel supremacy... parading the eminence of character

Distinction with features and visional promises of

A beautiful queen to be... for she was yet still young but

The wisest of women to see...

Suddenly, the mysticism of her exotic movements ceased

As heaven and earth stood still in solemn peace

As a pillowing cloud appeared before her like a cast of

A wish from heaven's Golden gates of divinity...

Stepping out of the cloud a man came forwardly

And for Some reason of intent fate or reality

The man in his wonder of splendor and gloriousness

Of etiquette was of a perfect resemblance of me...

He took the long black and red ribbon hat from his

Wave of hair and held it in his diamond ring of hand

Then, called the name Mari Adore like a mission man

And with a voided element of surprise

And the dazzling brightness of her triangularly painted eyes

157

Revealed an instant of recognition to an invitation

Of her dreamed moment of revelation

She blew the magic angel dust of

Golden crystal sand until it blew no more

And she watched it soar into the air of wistfulness

And made the final cast of wishfulness...

Let this day be cherished and adored

As the essence of a story told in accord

With many dreams which have come true

Let this story be a dream from me to you,

Like stories told of famous tales,

Pretty mermaids and sea fish shells,

Tall tales of wishing wells and voyages of the sea,

Time machines, odyssey inventions,

Unforgettable tales of great superstitions,

Black Friday and Friday the 13th

Don't let a pole come between you and your shadow

Seven years of bad luck for breaking a looking glass

Never let a black cat cross your path

Tell this story as a song and as you sing it pass it on

For the wise do know that the words a flow in fairy tales

Do hold true... and one day someone is going to sing a song

In the epic of a poem and pass a fairy tale on to you.

The saxophone began to play a jagged rhythm to say

The meaning that words sometimes fail to convey

The spirit in its depth of sound

Projects the love that has been found

Between two people from different worlds

Man, woman, boy and girl.

She went quickly to his open arms

As he whispered in her ear with sweet breath of charm

Tasting the perfume of her love with a tenderly plant of kiss

Onto her lips of pucker as his gentle hands slipped onto her

Slender of waist and their bodies emphatically clashed

In warm embrace as instant love for one another

Gave path of light to dark discover...

They sang and danced to the vigorously lazy beat of song

With joyous laughter and childish fun

And still the mellow tone of the saxophone as the

Whistling caress of musical wind sooth their flailing limbs

Into inner winding rhythm and harmony of tune

And the two connecting bodies reflected a silhouette

Under the florescent of moon from place to place

In odyssey of space across an illuminated sphere of galaxy

They took a chance with dance and romance

To a delightful flow and effervescent rhythm of a steady pace

With poetic rhyme, a fantasy of a beautiful moment of

Life and time and soon their shadows disappeared into a long

And dark stretch of zodiac hemisphere onto the yellow

And beautiful sun...Their new way of life had just begun

They sailed in a carriage led by white winged Stallion horses

Across a westerly sea under a darkened sky given

Eastern bound to arise in each other's arms with the sun

Into a perfect world of paradise where happiness peace

And love evolves as one... Their bright day is here.

Their dark days are done...Forevermore.

Index

Of Poems, Lyrics, Raps and Songs

Made in the USA
Charleston, SC
20 December 2015